The Newfoundland

by
Jo Ann Riley
and
Betty McDonnell

Compiled and Edited by
William W. Denlinger and R. Annabel Rathman

Cover Design by
Bob Groves

DENLINGER'S PUBLISHERS, LTD.
Box 76, Fairfax, Virginia 22030

Library of Congress Cataloging in Publication Data

Riley, Jo Ann.
  The Newfoundland.

  1. Newfoundland dogs. I. McDonnell, Betty.
II. Denlinger, William Watson.
III. Rathman, R. Annabel. IV. Title.
SF429.N4M36 1985   636.7′3   84-14211
ISBN 0-87714-110-X

International Standard Book Number: 0-87714-110-X

Acknowledgements

We are grateful to all the Newfoundland owners whose dogs are shown on the following pages for sharing their pictures, some of which are treasured "only copies."

We also wish to thank the following for their contributions of photographs, information, and assistance which helped make this book possible: Betty Barton, Gladys Craig, Mary Dewey, Kitty Drury, Peggy Helming, Karen Horst, Dena Hughes, Nita Jager, Linda Laughlin, Maree Lerchen, Karen McCashin, *Newf Tide*, Alex Polson, and Jane Thibault. Also, the Newfoundland Club of Seattle, and Sunset Magazine.

Jo Ann Riley
and
Betty McDonnell

Co-authors Jo Ann Riley (above), shown here with American and Canadian Ch. Seamount Jonah of Pouch Cove, and Betty McDonnell (below).

Reproduced on the front cover of this book is a photograph of the Newfoundland puppy Kilyka's Morgan and the dog Ch. Kilyka's Colossus, U.D., W.R.D., with David Goff, whom Colossus has just "rescued." (Photograph by Stephenie Koplin.)

Reproduced on the back cover (above) is a photograph of Ch. Halirock's Seamount Hannah and Seamount Whaleboat Teddy, fording a river while wearing backpacks. And (below) is a photograph of a puppy getting a ride in a kayak as his mother keeps him company. Both puppy and dam are Halirock Newfs owned by Roger and Jean Foster.

"A Distinguished Member of the Humane Society." Original painting by Sir Edwin Henry Landseer, the celebrated English artist, hangs in the National Gallery in London.

Contents

A dog train at Winnipeg, Canada.

Ch. Seaward's Blackbeard, being presented with the Best-in-Show award at the Westminister Kennel Club show, 1984. Owner, Seaward Kennels. Handler, Gerlinde Hockla. Judge, Mrs. Maynard K. Drury.

The Newfoundland

Gentle, benevolent, sweet; there are few accounts of the Newfoundland which do not include such words. These characteristics, combined with an impressive size, make the Newfoundland, or "Newf," as he is affectionately called, a most appealing creature. A bear-like appearance adds to his charm—he is the teddy bear of one's childhood come to life.

Adult Newfoundlands generally range in weight between 110 and 160 pounds, although extremes may go in either direction. Height ranges from twenty-four to thirty-two inches at the shoulder. Males, in general, are taller and heavier than bitches.

Black or Landseer (white with black markings) are the preferred coat colors, according to the Newfoundland Standard. Gray, brown, and other solid colors are acceptable. White markings on chest, toes, and tip of the tail are acceptable on dogs of a solid color. Markings other than white on solid color dogs, and coats of mixed color, are disqualified under the Newfoundland Standard.

The Newf is as amiable to live with as he appears upon first acquaintance. Newfs love people and thrive on human companionship. A Newf will not obviously attach himself to a single member of the family. If he has a preference, he still responds to others with warmth and affection. This quality makes the Newf a highly adaptable breed. Puppies and adult dogs usually adjust easily to loving new homes.

Any heavy-coated breed prefers a cool climate, but Newfs can adapt to heat. The coat of black Newfs absorbs the sun's heat very quickly. In hot climates they tend to shed the insulating undercoat permanently. Shade and cool drinking water are essential in hot weather.

Newfs, and indeed most mammals, tend to be inactive in hot weather. But under most conditions this agreeable dog will be active or inactive according to his owner's pleasure. The owner, in turn, is responsible for seeing that the dog gets sufficient exercise appropriate to his age, conditioning, and the weather.

Along with his agreeable nature, the Newf is probably best known for his swimming ability. He does not dog paddle, but swims with long strokes. The body lies almost parallel to the surface of the water as the dog swims, with the hindquarters only slightly lower in the water than the forequarters. The head may be held up out of the water, but many Newfs, especially when swimming just for fun, gulp water as they move along. Others squeak or whine, apparently in pleasure, for this is a trait of some of the most enthusiastic Newfie swimmers.

Some Newfs have a stronger desire to swim than do others. Often this is the result of early exposure to water. Most young puppies will enter water and begin swimming with little or no encouragement. A dog introduced to water at an older age may require coaxing and encouragement. Sometimes these late starters become among the greatest enthusiasts.

One bitch, not exposed to water until a camping trip at the age of nine months, refused to swim even though another Newf took every opportunity to cool himself in the frigid mountain rivers. The bitch would wade in but go no further, despite sticks being thrown for the dogs to retrieve, a favorite competitive sport on land.

On the trip home, the heat was intense. When her owners found a lake with a temperature tolerable to humans, they plunged in, accompanied by the male Newf. This was too much for the bitch. Perhaps she couldn't stand being left out, or feared for her owners' safety; in any event, she jumped in, swam out to her owners, and circled them repeatedly. This bitch became an outstanding swimmer who loved the water.

The circling behavior demonstrated by this bitch is typical of Newfoundlands swimming with humans. It appears to be a protective response born of a natural instinct for water rescue. It is curious that an animal so at home in the water should recognize the vulnerability of humans in this element and should fear for their safety.

Ch. Amity's Bearfoot of Pouch Cove, multiple Best-of-Breed winner, Group placer, influential stud dog in the eighties. Breeders, Diane Broderick and Peggy Helming. Owners, Peggy and David Helming.

Ch. Skipjack's Buddha of Fathom, a brown Newf bred by Ken and Terry Crawford and owned by Susan and Ralph Gesler. Buddha is the first brown Newf to win an all-breed Best-in-Show award.

American and Canadian Ch. Shipway's Knight Patrol, American and Canadian U.D.T., W.R.D., bred by Ann Sher and owned by Claire Carr. Knight is the most titled dog in the history of the breed.

It is a common experience for parents of young children to see their Newfs station themselves between the children and the water's edge. Some Newfs try to herd swimming children from the water, or hover closely as self-appointed life guards. Adult swimmers complain that their activities are hampered by their anxious Newfs, who insist upon circling or staying close.

Why have Newfoundlands plunged into the water to rescue friends or strangers when water holds no threat to the dogs themselves? It is a marvelous mystery which demands no solution.

Newfies have a great need for human attention. They can be kept successfully as kennel dogs with other dog companions, but each Newf needs human contact, attention, and, ideally, some work or training on a regular basis.

Probably the most content Newfs are those that live with their owners as house pets. They are stimulated by the coming and going of the family and guests, are talked to and petted frequently, and, above all, are with the people they love.

A Newf can be kept as an outdoor dog in a fenced yard with room to explore and exercise, but needs frequent owner contact, including walks, play, training, rides in the car, and grooming. Being left alone without such attention is unfair to the dog. Another Newf or dog companion is ideal when working owners are gone all day.

No dog should be chained, or allowed to run loose. Before choosing a dog as a pet, would-be owners should evaluate their commitments to owning a dog. If there is any doubt about being willing to meet its needs, they should opt for a less demanding pet.

As a house dog, the Newf has certain disadvantages. The dog will carry into the house—on coat, mouth, and feet—dust, rain, mud, and outdoor debris such as grass clippings and leaves. They also shed profusely at times, and some drool. Newfs are sloppy eaters and drinkers. Puppies may paddle in their water bowls or drink with one foot in the bowl. Most of these annoyances can be dealt with (suggestions will be found in later chapters), but a Newf is not for the fastidious housekeeper nor for one whose clothes must be immaculate at all times.

While the disadvantages of a Newf as house dog are mere annoyances, the advantages are invaluable. You need never come home to an empty house. There is nothing like the unabashed joy of a Newf's greeting to lift your spirits as well as to offer assurance that all is well. A dog is never judgmental. He offers love and trust in the worst of times as well as in the best.

Although the Newfoundland is not considered a guard dog, he does have a strong protective instinct. If a family is asleep or away from home, the Newf acts as a protector of the household. His deep bark alone will deter all but the most determined intruders.

A Newf is friendly toward guests, but when the door is opened to a stranger, a Newf can sense the "Who are you and what do you want?" attitude of his owner. He remains aloof until the owner's demeanor indicates trust. Even then, he can often sense when something is not right. If a Newf does not relax his aloof stance after the owner indicates acceptance of a stranger, there is reason to rely on his doubt.

The costs of maintaining any dog over its lifetime far exceed the purchase price of the dog. Newfies, like most giant breeds, are not inexpensive to buy and maintain. Feeding costs are quite reasonable, but supplies, equipment, and veterinary fees are higher than for smaller breeds. This is not to suggest that owning a Newfoundland is a formidable expense, but maintenance costs and unforeseen expenses should be included in the budget when planning to add a Newf to the family.

Ch. Dryad's Anthony's Penelope, bred by James Bellows and owned by Joan and Roger Foster.

The Tibetan Mastiff, a possible ancestor of the Newfoundland.

An old pen and ink drawing showing a Newf in a boat. Artist and source unknown.

The History of the Newfoundland

The origin of the Newfoundland is unknown. It is neither an ancient breed, as is the Saluki, of which there are pictorial records dating back seven thousand years, nor is it a fairly recently created breed such as the Doberman Pinscher, which dates from about 1890.

Over centuries, and even within centuries, breeders have changed certain characteristics of their various breeds, so that many dogs that appear in old illustrations are barely comparable to their contemporary counterparts. The present Newf resembles pictures of the old Tibetan Mastiff more than it does many of the early Newfoundland specimens identified in illustrations.

References to what appears to be a Newfoundland date back to the early 1600s, but the breed was not named until about 1775 when a George Cartwright referred to his own dog as a Newfoundland. A few years later the English naturalist Bewick gave a description of an English Newfoundland, along with its measurements and an illustration. The picture showed a black and white dog, of the type now known as the Landseer Newfoundland.

One theory of the Newfoundland's origin holds that large bear-like dogs, descended from the Tibetan Mastiff, were brought to the Eastern shores of the New World by the Norsemen in their early explorations. Another theory suggests that the Newf is a descendant of Tibetan Mastiffs that crossed the Bering Strait land bridge from Asia to North America. A third theory proposes that the Newf was a result of interbreeding among a native dog or dogs and the Great Pyrenees dogs brought to America by Basque fishermen.

There seems to be no favored theory on the Newfoundland's ancestors, but most authorities agree that the breed originated on the large island province in Eastern Canada that gave it its name.

The question of origin also involves whether the black type and the black and white Landseer type were originally two different breeds. Some Landseer owners maintain that their dogs have specific character traits that are different from those of the all-black Newfoundlands. Whether this lends credence to the theory that they evolved from different breeds is difficult to assess, because the black and the Landseer types have been interbred for many years.

Although the Newfoundland originated in North America, the breed prospered in England. During the late 1700s a law was passed in Newfoundland forbidding ownership of more than one family dog. The Newf population diminished on the island, and it was not until the early 1900s that the breed was revived in its homeland through the efforts of the Honorable Harold MacPherson, at his Westerland Kennels.

Meanwhile, in England the breed was being perpetuated and, with selective breeding, became recognized as purebred. The breed began to flourish about the turn of the century, becoming a favorite pet and children's companion. Sentimental pictures from the Victorian era often pictured a child and a Newf.

The foundation of today's Standard for the breed traces back to the type established in England in the dog Siki. Three Siki sons were imported into the United States. Ch. Harlingen Neptune and Ch. Seafarer, Siki sons owned by Elizabeth Loring Power of Waseeka Kennels, were dominant show winners of their time. They and their get became the foundation stock for the type found in present-day dogs.

Also considered foundation kennels for the present-day dogs were the Coastwise Kennels of Beatrice and Major Godsol, the Dryad Kennels of Maynard and Kitty Drury, and the Little Bear Kennels of Vadim and Margaret Chern. These breeders produced dogs of excellent type during a period when the Newf was a rare breed and almost unknown outside of the dog fancy. The successful kennels of today have made use of the heritage from the "pioneers" who maintained and enhanced the breed during difficult times.

Despite a lack of evidence to support a single theory of origin, there is no lack of information concerning the breed's existence since Bewick's time. Historical records, art, and literature document the Newfoundland's past.

Probably the most famous Newfoundland in American history is the dog Scannon, who accompanied Lewis and Clark on their 1804–1809 exploration of the American West. Scannon is mentioned a number of times in the journals of the expedition and is credited with saving the men from a buffalo. Lewis' entry for May 29, 1805, is as follows:

"Last night we were all alarmed by a large buffalo bull which swam over from the opposite shore and, coming along the side of the white pirogue, climbed over it to land. He, then alarmed, ran up the bank in full speed directly toward the fires, and was within 18 inches of the heads of some of the men who lay sleeping, before the sentinel could alarm him or make him change his course. Still more alarmed, he now took his direction immediately toward our lodge, passing between 4 fires, and within a few inches of the heads of one range of the men as they yet lay sleeping.

"When he was near the tent, my dog saved us by causing him to change his course a second time, which he did by turning a little to the right, and was quickly out of sight, leaving us by this time all in an uproar with our guns in our

Ch. Waseeka's Square Rigger, bred from Mrs. Davieson Power's Siki stock. Mrs. Power was instrumental in revitalizing the Newfoundland in the United States in the 1920s.

American, Canadian, Bermudian Ch. Newton, bred by the Honorable Harold McPherson. Mr. McPherson, of Westerlund Kennels in Newfoundland, revitalized the breed in Canada in the early 1900s. Newton won eleven Best-in-Show placements, and was Best of Breed at the 1965 and 1966 NCA National Specialties. He was in his heyday when AKC Newfoundland registrations began to increase.

hands, inquiring of each other the cause of the alarm, which, after a few moments, was explained by the sentinel. We were happy to find no one hurt."[1]

Sir Edwin Landseer immortalized the Newfoundland in his paintings. His best known Newf painting, "A Distinguished Member of the Humane Society," painted in 1837, features the black and white dog which was later named, and still is referred to as, the Landseer.

The well known painting, "Madame Charpentier and Her Children," by Auguste Renoir, shows a child seated on a Newfoundland, also a Landseer.

From the Victorian era, many paintings by lesser artists and prints by Currier and Ives can be found in antique shops and attics, attesting to the popularity of the Newfoundland in that period.

Lord Byron, the English poet, immortalized his beloved Newf, Boatswain, in the following eulogy, a most moving tribute to the character of a Newfoundland:

Near this Spot
are deposited the Remains of one
who possessed Beauty without Vanity,
Strength without Insolence,
Courage without Ferocity,
and all the Virtues of Man without his Vices.

This praise, which would be unmeaning Flattery
if inscribed over human Ashes,
is but a just tribute to the Memory of
BOATSWAIN, a DOG,
who was born in Newfoundland May 1803
and died at Newstead Nov. 18th, 1808

Nana, the Newfoundland nursemaid in James Barrie's *Peter Pan,* surely was inspired by the Newf's natural "tending" instinct:

"It was a lesson in propriety to see her escorting the children to school, walking sedately by their side. . . ." "She proved to be quite a treasure of a nurse. How thorough she was at bath time." "On John's soccer days she never once forgot his sweater, and she usually carried an umbrella in her mouth in case of rain."[2]

Though whimsical, the description of Nana's behavior toward her charges carries a strong element of truth.

In addition to *Peter Pan,* there are a number of children's books featuring Newfoundlands. A few are currently available; others can be found only through dealers of discontinued publications. Some titles are:

Sailor's Choice, by Natalie Carson
The Sorely Trying Day, by Russell Hoban
Pierre Pidgeon, by Lee Kingman
The Dog Crusoe, by R. M. Ballantine
Along Came a Dog, by Mindert de Jong (The dog in this story is not identified as a Newfoundland, but the illustrations and behavior of the dog strongly suggest a Newf.)

There is a wide range of Newfoundland memorabilia ranging from penny banks and figurines to postage stamps. Collectors can find antiques and replicas of antiques. A wide variety of Newf items also are available from the Newfoundland Club of America. Many of these items have been designed and produced by artists and craftsmen belonging to the club who, like their counterparts of the past, are helping to perpetuate the history of the breed through art.

[1]*The Journals of Lewis and Clark,* The New American Library, 1964.
[2]*Peter Pan*, James Barrie, Chas. Scribner and Sons, 1950.

The label on the back of this print, though damaged, indicates that the print may have been a premium for subscribing to *American Homes.* The label is dated 1872.

Antique brass bank in form of Newf with backpack.

Stamps picturing the Newf, from the islands of St. Pierre, Miquelon, and Newfoundland.

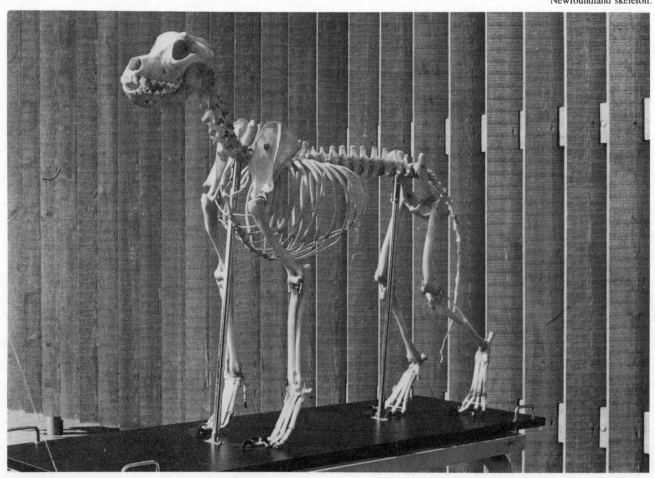

The Newfoundland Standard

All breeds recognized by The American Kennel Club as being eligible for registration have a written Standard describing an ideal specimen of the breed. The Standard is used by breeders to maintain the characteristics of their breeds. Dog show judges are required to know the Standards for the breeds they judge, and are expected to select as winners the dogs who most closely match the Standard.

The current Newfoundland Standard was written by the Newfoundland Club of America and was approved by the AKC in 1979.

Official Standard for the Newfoundland

General Characteristics & Appearance—The Newfoundland is a sweet-dispositioned dog that never acts either dull or ill-tempered. His expression is soft and reflects the characteristics of the breed—benevolence, intelligence, and dignity. He is a multi-purpose dog that is at home on land and in the water; he is capable of draft work and he possesses natural lifesaving instincts. He is a devoted companion to man and child.

He is large, heavy coated, well boned, strong, and appears to be square, although he is slightly longer than he is tall. He is balanced, deep bodied, and well muscled. A good specimen of the breed has dignity and proud head carriage. The dog's appearance is more massive throughout than the bitch's.

Head—The head is massive, with a broad skull, slightly arched crown, and strongly developed occipital bone. The slope of the stop is moderate but, because of well developed superciliary ridges, may appear abrupt in profile. The forehead and face are smooth and free of wrinkles. The muzzle is clean-cut and covered with short, fine hair. The muzzle is broad and deep; its length from the tip of the nose to the stop is less than that from the stop to the occiput. The top of the muzzle, when viewed from the front, is rounded. The bridge of the muzzle, when viewed from the side, is straight or only slightly arched. The nostrils are well developed.

The teeth meet in a scissors or level bite.

The eyes are dark brown, relatively small, deep-set and spaced wide apart. Eye color other than brown is very objectionable. The eyelids fit closely with no inversion.

The ears are relatively small and triangular with rounded tips. They are set well back on the skull, level with or slightly above the superciliary ridges, and lie close to the head. When the ear is brought forward, it reaches to the inner corner of the eye on the same side.

Neck & Body—The neck is strong and well set on the shoulders. It is long enough for proud head carriage. The topline is level from the withers to the croup. The back is broad, strong, and well muscled from the shoulders through the croup. The chest is full and deep with the brisket reaching at least down to the elbows. The croup slopes at an angle of about 30 degrees. The tail set follows the natural line of the croup. The tail is broad at the base and strong. The tail bones reach to the hock. When the dog is standing relaxed, its tail hangs straight or with a slight curve at the end. When the dog is in motion or excited, the tail is carried straight out or slightly curved, but it never curls over the back. A tail with a kink is objectionable.

Forequarters—The forelegs are well muscled and well boned. When the standing dog is viewed from the front, the forelegs are straight and parallel from the shoulder point to the ground, with the elbows pointing directly to the rear. The shoulders are well muscled. The layback of the shoulder blade is about 45 degrees and the upper arm meets the shoulder blade at an angle of about 90 degrees. The pasterns are strong and slightly sloping.

Hindquarters—The rear assembly is powerful, well muscled, and well boned. The croup is broad. When the standing dog is viewed from the rear, the legs are straight and parallel. Viewed from the side, the thigh is fairly long, the stifle well bent and the line from the hock to the ground is perpendicular to the ground.

Feet—The feet are proportionate to the body in size, cat-foot in type, well-rounded and tight with firm, arched toes. Complete webbing is always present.

Coat—The adult Newfoundland has a water-resistant, double coat. The outer coat is coarse, moderately long and full. It is straight and flat, although it may have a slight wave. The coat, when rubbed the wrong way, tends to fall back into place. An open coat is objectionable. The undercoat, which is soft and dense, is often less dense during the summer months or in tropical climates. The hair on the face and muzzle is short and fine. Excess hair on the ears may be trimmed. The legs are feathered all the way down. Feet may be trimmed for neatness. The tail is covered with long, dense hair, but it does not form a flag.

Color—The Newfoundland colors to be preferred are black or white and black (Landseer). A slight tinge of bronze in a black coat is acceptable as is white on the chin, chest, toes, and tip of tail on a black dog. The Landseer is a white dog with black markings. Typical Landseer markings are a black head with white on the muzzle and/or white blaze (or a black head), and black central body markings and black on the rump extending on to the tail. Excessive ticking is

American and Canadian Ch. Benham Knoll's Amy, bred by Philip Knowlton and owned by Vickie and Vic Nebeker. Amy was a Regional Specialty Best-of-Breed winner in 1978 and a Best-of-Opposite Sex winner in 1982.

Ch. Canoochee De Nashau-Auke, shown taking his third Best-in-Show win from the Veteran's Class at Midwest Regional Specialty, 1977. "Chinook" was bred and owned by Jane and Ron Thibault.

undesirable. Beauty of markings should be taken into consideration, but never at the expense of type and soundness. Solid colors other than black are acceptable. The following colors are disqualified: Brindle; merle; tri-color; any color other than white on a solid color dog; and any color other than black on a white dog.

Gait—The Newfoundland in motion has good reach, strong drive, and gives the impression of effortless power. Essential to good movement is the balance of correct front and rear assemblies. The forelegs and hindlegs travel straight forward and do not swing in an arc or move in and out in relation to the line of travel. As the dog's speed increases, the legs angle in from the shoulders and hips toward the center line of the body and tend toward single tracking. When moving, a slight roll of the skin is characteristic of the breed.

Size—The average height for adult dogs is 28 inches and for adult bitches, 26 inches. The approximate weight of adult dogs is 130 to 150 pounds, of adult bitches 100 to 120 pounds. Large size is desirable, but never at the expense of balance, structure and correct gait.

Structural and movement faults common to all working dogs are as undesirable in the Newfoundland as in any other breed, even though they are not specifically mentioned herein.

The foregoing description is that of the ideal Newfoundland. Any deviation from this ideal is to be penalized to the extent of the deviation.

Disqualifications—The following colors are disqualified: Brindle; merle; tri-color; any color other than white on a solid-colored dog; and any color other than black on a white dog.

Approved May 8, 1979
The Newfoundland Club of America

Ch. Companionway's Windjammer, bred by Fred Holt and owned by Connie Holt. "Jammie" was Best of Opposite Sex at the 1977 NCA National Specialty, and has all-breed Best-in-Show wins and multiple Group placements.

American and Canadian Ch. Topmast's Pied Piper, a Landseer bred and owned by Margaret Willmott. Piper was Best of Breed at the 1976 NCA National Specialty and is a multiple all-breed Best-in-Show winner.

Ch. Mogen of Newton-Ark, Best-of-Breed winner at the 1983 NCA National Specialty. Owned by Janet Levine and handled by Alan Levine.

Ch. Ferryland's Abby of Newton-Ark, Best-of-Opposite Sex winner at the 1983 NCA National Specialty. She also won the Brood Bitch and Veteran's Classes. Bred by Doris Swan, owned by Janet Levine, and handled by Dawn Chandler.

The Newfoundland Club of America

The Newfoundland Club of America (N.C.A.) was formed in 1930. Since its founding it has grown to include over fifteen hundred individual members representing thirteen countries.

The first American Newfoundland Standard, approved in 1930, was simply an adoption of the English Standard. A new Standard was approved in 1970, which served until 1979 when the latest revision was approved.

The N.C.A.'s concern with protecting and improving the Newfoundland is demonstrated by its activities and programs. A quarterly publication, *Newf Tide,* contains articles on health, breeding, working activities, and other educational material. The magazine also serves to keep members up to date on board meetings, upcoming events, Newfs that have earned new titles, and the activities of members.

Standing committees concerned with breed welfare include the Hip Dysplasia, Obedience, Standard, and Working Committees. An *ad hoc* committee currently is conducting a survey on the longevity of Newfoundlands.

Club publications are available for those interested in training their Newfs for water and draft work. There is also a wide range of Newfoundland books and novelties available through the club.

The N.C.A. is a member of The American Kennel Club, with a delegate who represents the club at AKC delegate meetings. The N.C.A. is also licensed by the AKC to hold Newfoundland Specialty Shows.

Nineteen regional clubs are sanctioned by the N.C.A. These clubs function autonomously under By-Laws approved by the N.C.A. They have the same concerns as the parent club but also deal with regional concerns and interests. Members have the opportunity to meet, share problems and information, and enjoy activities on a regular basis. Regional clubs may be approved by the parent club to host N.C.A. Regional Specialty Shows and Water Tests.

For Newf fanciers the highlight of the year is the National Specialty Show. This is usually a three-day event held in the spring. The show is hosted by one of the regional clubs and is rotated so that it is held in a different region each year.

The first National Specialty was held in 1933 in conjunction with the Morris and Essex Kennel Club in Madison, New Jersey. The first independently held National Specialty took place in Lenox, Massachusetts, in 1967. Since that date all but one or two National Specialties have been held independently. Entries have increased from 117 in 1967 to between 350 and 500 dogs at the more recent shows. Newfoundland fanciers from the fifty states and from as far away as Europe and Australia have the opportunity to meet together and enjoy watching the best Newfs currently competing in conformation, obedience, water work, and carting. In addition, Puppy Sweepstakes offer an opportunity for exhibition of young Newfs under eighteen months of age, and Junior Showmanship offers an exhibition of the handling abilities of young fanciers under eighteen years of age.

The increase in entries at the National Specialty Shows has paralleled the increase in breed registrations. Until the mid-1960s the Newfoundland was a little-known breed. About that time there was a growth in interest in all purebred dogs. AKC individual registrations rocketed from about 443,000 in 1960 to over 1,000,000 in 1970. Newfoundland registrations also began an upward swing. In 1963 about 260 Newfs were registered; in 1965, 571 Newfs were registered, and by 1970 there were 1,557 registrations. Growth leveled off in the 1970s and generally has remained at a little over 2,000 registrations per year. Records for 1984 show 2,297 registrations.

Excessive popularity, or becoming popular as a "fad breed," is never desired by those interested in the future of their breed. Popularity encourages indiscriminate breeding for commercial purposes by "puppy mills" and pet owners. Since the early 1970s the Newfoundland has maintained a comfortable position (about fiftieth) in the AKC registration rankings of 128 recognized breeds. The Newfoundland has come into its own as a breed widely recognized and admired without having faced the hazards of popularity.

Information regarding the Newfoundland Club of America, club publications, and the Breeders List may be obtained by writing the Corresponding Secretary of the N.C.A. The current Secretary's name and address is available from The American Kennel Club, 51 Madison Avenue, New York, New York, 10010.

Stud Dog Class judging at a 1982 NCA Regional Specialty.

Newfoundland Club of America
National Specialty Winners, 1940–1983

(BOB indicates Best of Breed winner; BOS indicates Best of Opposite Sex winner.)

YEAR		DOG	JUDGE
1940	(BOB)	Ch. Barnacle Bill of Waseeka (D)	Mrs. Bea Godsol
1941–1947*			
1948	(BOB)	Ch. Waseeka's Jolly Sailor Boy (D)	Mr. Alva Rosenberg
	(BOS)	Dryad's Coastwise Showboat (B)	
1950	(BOB)	Topsail's Captain Cook (D)	Mr. James Trullinger
	(BOS)	Oquaga's Queen Bess (B)	
1951	(BOB)	Ch. Bonnavista (B)	Mrs. G. Dodge
	(BOS)	Can. Ch. Topsail's Captain Cook (D)	
1952	(BOB)	Ch. Dryad's Coastwise Showboat (B)	Mrs. Francis Crane
	(BOS)	Dryad's Decorative Accessory (D)	
1953	(BOB)	Waseeka's Ghostship (D)	Mr. Alva Rosenberg
	(BOS)	Ch. Dryad's Coastwise Showboat (B)	
1954	(BOB)	Ch. Little Bear's Big Chance (D)	Mrs. Frank Butcher
	(BOS)	Ch. Bonnavista (B)	
1955	(BOB)	Ch. Waseeka's Ghostship (D)	Mr. Albert VanCourt
	(BOS)	Ch. Waseeka's Zanzibar (B)	
1956	(BOB)	Ch. Pretty's Terra Nova (B)	Mrs. Bea Godsol
	(BOS)	Ch. Waseeka's Indianman (D)	
1957	(BOB)	Ch. Sea Captain (D)	Mr. Maynard Drury
	(BOS)	Ch. Perivale Elinor of Aquitaine (B)	
1958	(BOB)	Ch. Little Bear's Canicula Campio (D)	Mr. Ted Gunderson
	(BOS)	Little Bear's Ocean Borne (B)	
1959	(BOB)	Ch. Harobed's Hamish (D)	Mrs. E. Power
	(BOS)	Ch. Dryad's Lighthouse Beam (B)	
1960	(BOB)	Can. Ch. Eskimo's Grey Mug (D)	Mrs. Kitty Drury
	(BOS)	Harobed's Nancy of Moralview (B)	
1961	(BOB)	Ch. Little Bear's Caniculo Campio (D)	Mr. Ken C. Tiffin
	(BOS)	Dryad's Anguille (B)	
1962	(BOB)	Ch. Montana Mustang Arno (D)	Mr. Maynard Drury
	(BOS)	Tenamend Black Dolphin (B)	
1963	(BOB)	Ch. Captain Morgan's Prince (D)	Mrs. Francis Crane
	(BOS)	Dryad's Mistletoe (B)	
1964	(BOB)	Ch. Little Bear's Thunder, U.D. (D)	Mr. J. A. Cuneo
	(BOS)	Ch. Kwasind's Feather in Her Cap (B)	
1965	(BOB)	Int. Ch. Newton (D)	Mrs. Bea Godsol
	(BOS)	Ch. Harobed Hill's Magus of the Sea (B)	
1966	(BOB)	Int. Ch. Newton (D)	Mr. Major B. Godsol
	(BOS)	Ch. Dryad's Sea Rose (B)	
1967	(BOB)	Can. Ch. Edenglen's Banner (D)	Mrs. D. D. Power
	(BOS)	Ch. Dryad's Christmas Cheer (B)	
1968	(BOB)	Am. Can. Ch. Edenglen's Banner (D)	Mrs. Bea Godsol
	(BOS)	Ch. Hilvig's Corsage (B)	
1969	(BOB)	Ch. Tranquilus Betty of Subira (B)	Mr. Alva Rosenberg
	(BOS)	Shadyhollow's Jonathan (D)	
1970	(BOB)	Ch. Edenglen's Falstaff (D)	Mrs. C. S. Smith
	(BOS)	Ch. Edenglen's Heidi Bear (B)	

YEAR	DOG		JUDGE
1971	(BOB)	Ch. Kilyka's Jupiter Rex (D)	Mrs. Alva McColl
		(BOS) Ch. Niote of Newton-Ark (B)	
1972	(BOB)	Ch. Dryad's Tambaram of Cayuga (D)	Mrs. N. Demidoff
		(BOS) Ch. Dory-O's Seanymph of Bethward (B)	
1973	(BOB)	Ch. Indigo's Fritzacker (D)	Mrs. B. Gothen
		(BOS) Ch. Black Molly of Warren (B)	
1974	(BOB)	Ch. Canoochee de Nashua-Auke (D)	Mrs. V. Hampton
		(BOS) Ch. Shipshape's Windsong (B)	
1975	(BOB)	Ch. Ship Chandler's Sea Eagle (D)	Mr. John Cassevay
		(BOS) Ch. Riptide's Nantucket Lightship (B)	
1976	(BOB)	Am. Can. Ch. Topmast Pied Piper (D)	Mr. Terry Temple
		(BOS) Ch. Kilyka's Jessica of Pouch Cove (B)	
1977	(BOB)	Ch. DaCody de Nashua-Auke (D)	Mrs. N. Demidoff
		(BOS) Ch. Companionway's Winjammer (B)	
1978	(BOB)	Ch. Anestasia's Magic Marker (B)	Mr. M. Downing
		(BOS) Am. Can. Ch. Hornblower's Long John Silver (D)	
1979	(BOB)	Ch. Kilyka's Black Bart (D)	Mrs. Esther Mueller
		(BOS) Ch. Ferryland's Abby of Newton-Ark (B)	
1980	(BOB)	Ch. Pooh Bear's Stormalong (D)	Mr. Derek Rayne
		(BOS) Am. Can. Ch. Topmast Prairie Queen (B)	
1981	(BOB)	Ch. Britannia's Hurricane Jack (D)	Mr. Charles Visich
		(BOS) Ch. Tuckamore's Ely of Pouch Cove (B)	
1982	(BOB)	Am. Can. Ch. Seaward's Blackbeard (D)	Mr. Anthony Hodges
		(BOS) Ch. Edenglen's Bonne Bay (B)	
1983	(BOB)	Ch. Mogen of Newton Ark (D)	Mr. Joseph Gregory
		(BOS) Ch. Ferryland's Abby of Newton Ark (B)	
1984	(BOB)	Ch. Seaward's Blackbeard (D)	Mr. Glen Sommers
		(BOS) Ch. Diamond of Newton Ark (B)	
1985	(BOB)	Ch. Tuckamore's Julie (B)''	Mrs. Jo Ann Riley
		(BOS) Ch. Shadybrook's Late Arrival (D)	

*We can only assume that no Specialties were held between 1941 and 1947 because of World War II. We found that there was only one wartime Newf column, in 1943, in the AKC *Gazette*. In the April 1946 issue of the *Gazette,* Bea Godsol wrote "It was voted not to hold a Specialty Show this year because of the extensive breeding programs of various members. In spite of curtailment of Newfoundland activities during the war most breeders have been able to keep their bloodlines intact."

American and Canadian Ch. Dryad's Compass Rose, bred by Dryad Kennels and owned by Christine Lister. Rosie was a Group-placing bitch and an outstanding producer at the Shipshape Kennels of Wilma and Bob Lister.

National Specialty Highest Scoring Dog in Trial
(Dog's score in parentheses)

1968   Ch. Dryad's Lord Nelson, C.D. (192)
1969   (No passing score)
1970   Henna von Shartenberg, C.D. (187½)
1971   Ch. Dryad's Lord Nelson, U.D.T. (199½)
1972   Ebonewf's Hilarion (195½)
1973   Ch. Holiday's Dreadnought Ensign (194½)
1974   Rivendell's Cato (198)
1975   Britannia's OC Seven, C.D. (193)
1976   Dandie Lion Alum (194½)
1977   Turtleridge's Hildegarde (193½)
1978   Mt. Pleasant's Refraff Zealog, C.D.X. (196½)
1979   Briarcreek Barefoot Boy (196)
1980   Ch. Kilyka's Sea Shell, C.D.X. (192)
1981   Paddlewheel's Empress Lily (196)
1982   Can. OT Ch. Northtor's Lady Jane, C.D. (197½)
1983   Seaward's Fafner, Am. Can. C.D. (197½)
1984   Kilyka's Pollyanna (196)
1985   Kilyka's Pollyanna, C.D. (196)

National Specialty Top Junior Handler
(Handler and Dog)

1971   Jill Hall—Newfy's Creme de Cocoa
1972   Holly Balzer—Oronocah's Black Beary Sam
1973   Constance Holt—Ch. Companionway's Wind Pennant
1974   Holly Balzer—Ch. Oronocah's Black Beary Sam
1975   Elizabeth Kissel—Edenglen's Blackberry Tart
1976   Joanne McGovern—Ch. DeKoryak de Nashua-Auke
1977   Wendy Mackes—Moonlite Quasar
1978   Lisa Passonno—Ebonewf Boradaile's Lord Gus
1979   Sandy Cameron—Castaway's Tender Sheba
1980   Todd Thompson—Britannia's Brer Bear
1981   Jay Anderson—Dal-Ken's Swashbuckler
1982   Susan Woody—Hugybear's Sweet Magnolia
1983   Nancy Nebeker—Flying Cloud's Pooh Bear

1984   Joseph J. Reinisch, Jr.—Kudos Callisto of Seastar
1985   Susan Woody—Ch. Hugybear's Poppy

Ch. Flying Cloud's Silver Streak, a gray bitch bred and owned by Vickie and Vic Nebeker.

Ch. Motion Carried of Pouch Cove, bred and owned by David and Peggy Helming, was Winners Bitch at the 1982 National Specialty at just a few days over six months of age.

The N.C.A. Breeders List dates back to about the late 1960s. Prior to that time, breeders could list their litters with the Corresponding Secretary of the club. As the number of breeders increased, this system of referrals became quite cumbersome. It also put the Secretary in the position of referring prospective buyers to one or two breeders on the basis of proximity—whoever was closest to the prospective buyer.

Any breeder meeting the minimum requirements could be included on the Breeders List for the first few years it was published. As the list grew, it became obvious that anyone who could meet the minimum requirements listed their kennel even though they rarely had puppies for sale. Other persons were in Newfs for a while, then were never heard from again. In order to discourage these people from placing listings, the N.C.A. decided to charge a fee for listings, in addition to the minimum requirements listed below.

"The Newfoundland Club of America does not supervise or guarantee the ethical practices of these breeders, however the breeders listed below have met these minimal requirements:

1. Three year membership in the Newfoundland Club of America

2. Bred two litters while a member of the Newfoundland Club of America

3. Bred one litter during the past three years

The Newfoundland Club of America urges every prospective buyer of Newfoundlands to inform himself thoroughly before purchasing a dog."

In the listings below, the color bred by individual kennels is indicated by one or more asterisks following the kennel name, as follows: * indicates Landseer; ** indicates brown; *** indicates gray. If no asterisk appears following the kennel name, the kennel breeds black Newfoundlands only. If the kennel offers stud service, that fact is indicated by (S) following the kennel name.

Newfoundland Club of America, Inc.
Breeder and Stud Dog List, 1985–86

KENNEL NAME	OWNER(S)	LOCATION
Allison Acres* (S)	Connie Allison	Lunenburg, Massachusetts
Amity Newfoundlands	Diane and Tom Broderick	Ramsey, New Jersey
Aotea Newfoundlands (S)	Mrs. Gillian B. McArthur	Honeoye Falls, New York·
Apogee Kennels	Jerry and Betty Zarger	Westbrook, Connecticut
Aqua Knight Newfoundlands	Betty A. Windisch	Kent, Washington
Atlantis Kennel	Mildred J. Williams	Stanfordville, New York
Baranca Newfoundlands	Anne and Barney Weber	Lindenhurst, New York
Barharber Kennel (S)	David and Donna Barber	Downingtown, Pennsylvania
Belair Newfs**	Bill and Cathie Carl	Newmanstown, Pennsylvania
Bellisima Newfoundlands (S)	Joseph and Kerry Pecoraro	Oakdale, New York
Benhil Kennels* (S)	Joan and Paul Bendure	Fairview, Pennsylvania
Black Marsh Kennels** (S)	Paul and Muriel Levesque	Salisbury, Massachusetts
Bos'n Newfoundlands*	Richard and Ann Whitmore	Mountain Ranch, California
Briny Deep's Newfoundlands (S)	Claire Ives	North Troy, Vermont; Bantam, Connecticut
Brunhaus* **(S)	Verne and Carol Landt	Tok, Alaska
Callisto Newfoundlands* (S)	Susie Purvis	Corrales, New Mexico
Celtic Kennels (S)	Thomas and Nancy McGill	Williamstown, Massachusetts
Dalken	Ken and Dallas Anderson	Center, Colorado
Dirigo Newfoundlands**	Penny Gray Webb	Tucson, Arizona
Dryad Kennels, Reg. (S)	Mrs. Jay Dewey	Conifer, Colorado
Ebonewf** (S)	Roy and Louise Esiason	Granville, New York
Ebunyzar (S)	Hannah Hayman	Cazenovia, New York
Edenglen Kennels, Reg. (S)	Helena M. Linn	Dundee, New York
Evangeline Kennel (S)	Philip and Mary Lauer	Riegelsville, Pennsylvania
Ferromont Newfoundlands	Lynne Rutenberg	Mine Hill, New Jersey
Fireside	Dave and Kady Sturtz	Louisville, Colorado
Flying Cloud Newfoundlands (S)	Victor and Vickie Nebeker	Evergreen, Colorado
Halirock Kennels, Reg. (S)	Dr. and Mrs. Roger Foster, Jr.	Shelburne, Vermont

American and Canadian Ch. Seaward's Blackbeard, 1982 NCA National Specialty winner, bred by Nancy McMahon and owned by Seaward Kennels. "Adam" is the top winning Newfoundland in the history of the breed, with more than thirty Best-in-Show wins, and was the top Newf in the United States in 1981 and 1982. He was the Best-of-Breed winner in the Newfoundland National Specialty for two consecutive years—1983 and 1984.

American, Canadian, and Mexican Ch. Brittania's Hurricane Jack, 1981 NCA National Specialty winner, bred by Alana Manzer Shirley and Sydney Phelam and owned by Carol and Richard Whitmore. "Boomer" also is an all-breed Best-in-Show winner.

KENNEL NAME	OWNER(S)	LOCATION
Hannibal Kennels, Reg. (C.K.C.)	Peter and Maribeth Maniate	Toronto, Ontario, Canada
Hard Tack Newfoundlands (S)	D. C. and Georgia Basolo	Hillsborough California
Haven Hills (S)	Joyce Hieber	Wingdale, New York
Hugybear Kennel*	Ronald W. Woody	Woodstock, Illinois
Intrepid Newfoundlands (S)	Janice V. and Stuart I. Rixman	Weston, Connecticut
Jensfjord Farms (S)	Howard and Laura Jensen	Maple Plain, Minnesota
Jorgensen Colorado Newfoundlands* ***(S)	Roger and Donna Jorgensen	Longmont, Colorado
Kendian** (S)	Kendall and Diane Price	Los Gatos, California
Kilyka Newfoundlands	Mrs. Betty McDonnell	Mahwah, New Jersey
Lifeguard (S)	Joe and Claire Reinisch	Rancho Palos Verdes, California
Little Bear Kennels, Reg. (S)	Virginia M. Wooster	New Milford, Connecticut
Littlecreek Kennels, Reg. (C.K.C.)	Margaret Brown	Carlisle, Ontario, Canada
Mooncusser Newfoundlands	Suzanne Jones	Orleans, Massachusetts
Muddy Creek Newfoundlands* (S)	Rick and Brenda Santiago	Pearl River, New York
Nanwick (S)	Nancy Wick	Medina, Ohio
Nashau-Auke* (S)	Ronald and Jane Thibault	Ashford, Connecticut
Newfport (S)	May and Jack Bernhard	Putnam Valley, New York
Newmhoon Kennel	Marlla Mhoon	Maple Valley, Washington
Nine Mile Newfoundlands	Barton and Anne Williams	Bloomington, Minnesota
Northrop (S)	Marilyn V. Johnson	Minneapolis, Minnesota
Norwest (S)	Nancy Wheeler	Lakebay, Washington
Ottawa Newfoundlands	Consie and Roger Powell	Raleigh, North Carolina
Paddlewheel Newfoundlands (S)	Bob and Mary Price	Edina, Minnesota
Pandaga Newfoundlands (S)	Jacqueline Brellochs	Ithaca, New York
Peppertree* (S)	Penelope Freeman Stuckey	Olympia, Washington
Pioneer	Carole Cobb Granquist	Berlin, Wisconsin
Playguard** (S)	Jeanne Brelsford Bryson	Muncy, Pennsylvania
Poo Bear (S)	Pam Lovelove Gremillion	Memphis, Tennessee
Pouch Cove Newfoundlands (S)	Peggy and David Helming	Flemington, New Jersey
Proud Maji Kennel*	Susanne Pellegrino	East Haven, Connecticut
Rainbow Kennels (S)	Barbara Rouleau	Chino, California
Sandcastle** ***(S)	Saundra Harvey	Logan, Ohio
Seafaring Newfoundlands (S)	Christine and Allen Lawrence	Luxemburg, Wisconsin
Seaplay Newfoundlands (S)	Deborah and Roy Craig	Berlin, Maryland
Seaward Kennels, Reg.* (S)	Elinor Ayers	Manchester Center, Vermont
Seaworthy Newfoundlands (S)	Claire Carr and Ann Marie Torres	San Diego, California
Shadybrook Newfoundlands (S)	Richard and Jeri Krokum	Hillsboro, Oregon
Shiloh Newfoundlands (S)	Philip and Ellen Armstrong	Woodland, Pennsylvania
Skimeister Kennels* (S)	Debby and Dwight Summers	Glen Rock, Pennsylvania
Southwind Farms	Robin L. Seaman	Rehoboth, Massachusetts
Spillway Newfoundlands (S)	Phyllis Welch	Blanchard, Pennsylvania
Spring Harbor Newfoundlands* (S)	Ralph and Mary Averill	Holly, Michigan
Steamboat* (S)	Elizabeth Stackhouse	Snohomish, Washington
Sunnyside Newfoundlands* (S)	Jean and James Phipps	Sanderson, Texas
Sweetbay Newfoundlands*** (S)	Judi and Ellis Adler	Sherwood, Oregon
Tarbell Kennels	Ruth March	Livingston Manor, New York
Tatoosh	Maree E. Lerchen (Mrs. Thomas W.)	Packwood, Washington
T-Bar Newfoundlands*	Barbara Bathony	Anchorage, Alaska
The Munday Kennels (S)	R. Bowen and Helen D. Munday	South Salem, New York
Thunder Bay Newfoundlands**	Norman Belanger	Southfield, Michigan
Topmast	Mrs. Margaret Willmott	Pense, Saskatchewan, Canada

KENNEL NAME	OWNER(S)	LOCATION
Tranquilus Kennel, Reg. (S)	Capt. James Bellows, USNR, Ret., and Dorothea R. Bellows	Ft. Myers Beach, Florida; Sterling, New York
Tuckamore (S)	Barbara A. Finch	Pittstown, New Jersey
V. D. Uckermark	H. Kretschmer	Winterback, West Germany
Viking Newfoundlands (S)	Flip and Bill Bowser	Chillicothe, Ohio
Watchbear Newfoundlands	Jeanne and Terry Fashempour	Medina, Ohio
Welcove Kennel (S)	Candy and Fred D. Welch, Jr.	Bonneau, South Carolina
Windrift	Susan H. Woody	Crystal Lake, Illinois
Wittenberg Newfoundlands (S)	Chuck and Lynn Hughes	Batavia, New York
Yon Kennels (S)	Dana Yon Phillips and Terence B. Phillips	Alpharetta, Georgia
Zambuca Newfoundlands	Linda R. Becker	Parsippany, New Jersey
Z'Ourgang Newfs* (S)	Pattie Zielke	Los Gatos, California

The following is the 1971 N.C.A. Breeder's List. It is reprinted here for historical reference only, as a comparison to the 1983 list of breeders.

Newfoundland Club of America, Inc.
Breeder's List, 1971

KENNEL NAME	OWNER(S)	LOCATION
Adelbar Kennels, Reg.	Mrs. Mary Ann Smith	Chewelah, Washington
Almont's Newfs	Mr. and Mrs. Alfred Montgomery	Yaphank, New York
Alta View Kennels	Mr. and Mrs. Larry Holder	Sandy, Utah
Arcturus Kennels	Mrs. Christine Tutak	Los Angeles, California
Bandom Acres	Mrs. Mae Freeland	Sewickley, Pennsylvania
Barbara-Allen Kennels	Mrs. Allen Wolman	Bothell, Washington
Beaupre Newfoundlands	Mrs. E. A. Gleason, Jr.	Lenox, Massachusetts
Bethward Newfoundlands	Mr. Paul Ramey	Lemont, Illinois
Black Mischief Kennels	Mrs. Alice Weaver	Le Roy, Kansas
Black Watch Kennel	Mr. and Mrs. John Macaulay	West Boxford, Massachusetts
Brittania Kennels	Mrs. Alana S. Manzer	San Francisco, California
Cast Aways Kennel	Mr. and Mrs. Alan Maltby	Pinckney, Michigan
Companionway Kennel	Mr and Mrs. F. H. Holt	Warwick Neck, Rhode Island
David's Boarding and Breeding Kennel	Mr. David Swain	Mocksville, New York
Dory-O Kennels, Reg.	Mr. W. F. Cochrane	Delta, British Columbia, Canada
Ebonewf Kennels	Mr. and Mrs. Roy Esiason	East Northport, New York
Edenglen Kennels, Reg.	Mr. and Mrs. Willis Linn	Dundee, New York
Halirock Kennels, Reg.	Dr. and Mrs. Roger Foster, Jr.	Shelburne, Vermont
Harobed Hill Kennel	The Drs. Miller	San Dimas, California
Hilvig Kennels	Mrs. Hilda C. Madsen	Phillipsburg, New Jersey
Indigo Kennels	Mr. and Mrs. M. G. O'Neill	Rollingsford, New Hampshire
Irwindyl Kennels, Reg.	Mrs. Geraldine Irwin	Reading, Pennsylvania
Jensfjord Farm	Mr. and Mrs. H. C. Jensen	Norristown, Pennsylvania
Kilyka Newfoundlands	Mrs. George McDonnell	Ridgewood, New Jersey
Kimtale Kennels, Reg.	Mrs. A. R. MacKenzie	Ontario, Canada
Kodiak Kennels	Mr. and Mrs. Gene Wilson	Hiram, Ohio
Little Bear Kennels, Reg.	Mr. and Mrs. Vadim Chern	New Milford, Connecticut
Lynbel Kennels	Mr. R. F. Carpenter	Medina, Ohio
Meadow Moor Kennels	Barbara Moore	Elizaville, New York
Mylord Kennels	Mr. C. G. Cannell	Shaftsbury, Vermont
Nashua-Auke Kennel	Mr. and Mrs. Ronald Thibault	Mansfield Center, Connecticut

KENNEL NAME	OWNER(S)	LOCATION
Newfield Kennel	Mr. Joshua Loring, Jr.	Wrentham, Massachusetts
Newfman Kennel	Mr. Guy Campbell	Pawlet, Vermont
Newton-Ark Kennel	Mr. and Mrs. Alan Levine	Whitehouse Station, New Jersey
Oquaga Kennels, Reg.	Mr. and Mrs. Clifford Harts	Windsor, New York
Peppertree Kennels	Mr. and Mrs. W. E. Buell, Jr.	Cave Junction, Oregon
Pondameer Kennels	Mrs. Ann Larson	Port Byron, Illinois
Pouch Cove Newfoundlands	Mrs. David Helming	Whitehouse Station, New Jersey
Radcliffe Newfoundlands	Dr. and Mrs. R. R. MacMahon	No. Adams, Massachusetts
Ringfairn Kennels	Mr. and Mrs. J. K. Ring, Jr.	Roanoke, Virginia
Riptide Kennels	Mr. and Mrs. Grant Hoag	Northridge, California
Seamount Kennels	Mrs. Alan Riley	Mountlake Terrace, Washington
Seaward Kennels, Reg.	Mrs. Ralph Jameson	Montclair, New Jersey
Shaughrue's Kennels	Mr. J. E. Shockroo	So. Easton, Massachusetts
Shipshape Kennels	Mr. and Mrs. Robert Lister	West Barnstable, Massachusetts
Shipway Kennels	Dr. and Mrs. S. B. Scher	Montrose, Pennsylvania
Silverbrook Kennels	Mrs. Dorothy Durgin	Gorham, Maine
Sojowase Kennel	Mr. and Mrs. J. G. Schmoyer	Germansville, Pennsylvania
Topmast Kennel	Mrs. Margaret Willmott	Ontario, Canada
Tranquilus Kennel, Reg.	Capt. J. W. Bellows, Ret.	Fair Haven, New York
Wanaka Kennels	Mrs. Anne Moesch	Hamburg, New York
Windward Kennels	Mr. and Mrs. G. J. Fitzpatrick	Whitehouse Station, New Jersey
Wynfomeer Kennels	Mr. and Mrs. E. J. Cummings	Stone Ridge, New York
Zephyrus Newfoundlands	Mr. and Mrs. C. A. Beck	Costa Mesa, California

Best-of-Breed judging at the 1982 National Specialty.

Kilyka's Newmhoon tries to pull her young owner on a sled, without benefit of a harness. "Lady" was bred by Betty McDonnell and is owned by Marjla and Dave Mhoon.

"Dolly's Sleigh Ride." Courtesy Paula and Bob Bartak.

28

The Newfoundland Character

Humanity is enriched by the selflessness of heroic deeds. There is something especially touching about canine heroism when creatures, which we tend to view as dependent and somewhat childlike, demonstrate intelligence, creativity, and generosity beyond our expectations.

Newfoundland lore abounds with tales of heroism—some documented, others apocryphal.

Probably the most noted account of a Newf rescue occurred in 1919. The steamer *Ethie* had been flung against rocks during a storm along the coast of Nova Scotia. She began breaking up in the heavy swells. The lifeboats were washed away and one sailor was drowned in an attempt to reach shore with a line. As a last resort, after boats from shore failed to reach the vessel, the ship's Newfoundland was sent overboard. The dog, Tang, struggled ashore with a line in his mouth. This made possible the rigging of a boatswain's chair by which all passengers and crew were rescued. Tang was awarded a medal for his deed by Lloyds of London.

A number of years ago, when commonly asked if our Newfoundlands were black Saint Bernards, we encountered an older woman who identified our dog as a Newf. As we expressed pleasure and surprise at her recognition, she told us that she owed her life to a Newfoundland. Pressed for details, she said that she was very young when the rescue occurred, but she knew the story well because it had been told over and over within her family. She went on to explain that her family had made a trip by train from their home in Wisconsin to St. Paul, Minnesota to buy a Newf puppy from a pet store. The puppy grew up with the children and usually accompanied them in their play activities. One day the children and their Newf went to play by a mill pond near their rural home. The older children soon moved on to other activities while the woman and her younger brother stayed at the pond tossing in sticks. Somehow both children tumbled into the water. The deep pond, with its steep sides, made it impossible for them to climb out, and they began to shout. The Newfoundland, who had gone with the more active older group, heard the shouts, raced back to the pond, dived in, and supported the girl until her brothers and sisters arrived to pull her out. In the meantime, the younger brother had gone under. While one of the children ran for help, the

dog began diving for the boy. Even after a boat had been brought in to drag the pond, the Newf continued to dive until the boy was pulled out, drowned. The dog developed an ear infection as a result of his prolonged diving. Today he might have been saved, but with the treatment available at that time, the condition could not be cleared up and the dog had to be put to sleep.

One summer day a Seattle family took their six-month-old Newfoundland puppy to a lake for the first time. For about an hour, Tug played in the shallows discovering that he could swim. He was back on shore with the mother when his ten-year-old mistress rowed a small rubber boat out about forty feet from shore. Curious as to what the puppy's reaction would be, the mother cried, "Go get Annie, Tug!" Tug leaped into the water and began to swim to the boat. He looked back once, then swam straight for the boat where Annie held out a short painter for him to take. He grasped the line in his mouth and immediately headed for shore, somewhat concerned about the boat which was bumping him due to the shortness of the line. But he did not drop the line until the boat reached shore. The humans were aware that the child did not need to be rescued, but the inexperienced puppy did not know this. Despite the fact that he had learned to swim less than an hour earlier, he obeyed a command he had never been taught and towed to shore a boat which caused him some anxiety for his own safety.

In 1974, a bitch, Ursa, demonstrated this same instinct to "go to the rescue." Her mistress, who was summering on an island off the coast of Maine, left the mainland late one evening to return home. There was a heavy fog but with the aid of a flashlight she managed to maneuver her boat through those moored in the harbor. The island lay about a mile beyond the last boats and she intended to find her way by following familiar lobster markers. As the sea swells became higher, making the markers difficult to see, she realized she had overshot the island. To add to her predicament, the motor died. In desperation, she gave a frantic shout for help, then slumped in despair onto the seat. Shortly afterward, she became aware of a bark which was repeated every few seconds. She responded by calling her dog's name, guiding Ursa toward the boat. The dog apparently had heard the motor as the boat passed the island, then heard her mistress call after the motor died. When Ursa reached the boat, her owner threw out the bow line and the dog took it in her mouth. The woman made one last try to start the motor and it caught. Ursa swam ahead of the boat, leading the way to the mooring. Her heroic efforts were recognized at the 1976 Newfoundland National Specialty banquet, where she was awarded the Newfoundland Club of America's Achievement Award.

Early on a December morning in 1973, a well known Newfoundland breeder in Nova Scotia was awakened by the bark of Whaler, an eight-month-old puppy. The house was on fire! The woman roused her two young daughters.

One helped get all the dogs and a litter of puppies out of the house while the other ran for help. Whaler had been taken out with the other dogs but later ran back in, presumably to find the other child, who had gone for help. To their great sorrow, the family found that the puppy who had saved them with his alarm had perished in the house. They felt he had given his life in his attempt to save the girl.

Candy belonged to a couple in British Columbia. Their five-year-old son was playing outside with a friend one day while his father was pulling stumps in the yard with a bulldozer. The boy had been warned never to play anywhere near the machine. From the dining room, his mother and a family friend watched the bulldozer operation. It was backing up when her son appeared from nowhere, running toward the path of the bulldozer. He apparently was engrossed in some sort of game with a friend and was unaware that the machine was approaching. The mother, realizing that her husband, high in the seat, had no vision of anything close to the rear of the bulldozer, screamed and rushed outside to intervene. While she was out of sight of the boy, her friend, who was still watching out the window, saw Candy come from behind some trees and run headlong into the boy, pushing him out of the bulldozer's path. Both boy and dog were unharmed.

The deeds of many Newfoundlands have been filled with drama. Others have been simple responses to danger. Regardless of the circumstances, it is rewarding to realize that Newfoundland heroism and rescues are not simply tales from the past, but are an ongoing gift from this generous, loving breed to the human community.

The similarities between canines, wild and domestic, are greater than their differences. Thus a wolf and a Bulldog, for example, share the canine traits which identify them as members of a single species. Yet even among domestic dogs there are obvious differences. Selective breeding has resulted in genetic enhancement of certain canine traits and instincts desired in each breed, and in a diminution of traits considered less important. With its own genetic blueprint perpetuated over generations of controlled breeding, each breed has certain predictable traits which distinguish it from other breeds.

The Newfoundland breed is blessed with traits which make these dogs delightful and fascinating companions. A casual encounter reveals a Newfoundland's warmth. Living with a Newfoundland reveals his generosity, his wisdom, and his exceptional ability to communicate. The following experiences of Newfoundlands and Newf owners can better describe the character of the Newfoundland than any labels we might attach to him.

After dinner in Ripple's household there was no peace until she had her nightly walk. She would get her own lead, then badger her owner until he began moving toward the door. Until she was older she did not walk sedately, but tugged at the lead in the direction of anything which caught her interest. One evening she pulled her owner over to some brush near the edge of the sidewalk. She picked up something but her owner could not see what it was, because it was completely hidden in her mouth. Concerned that it might be a rotting bone or food, he stopped to pry open her mouth before she could eat it. Out hopped a fledgling, dry and unharmed.

Walking on lead with her owners' small granddaughter, Ripple never pulled nor tugged. If the toddler dropped the lead, as she usually did when bringing in the mail, the dog simply picked up the loose end of the lead and carried it in her mouth as she led the child back to the house.

Annie's family bought four six-week-old piglets. She became very excited over the little creatures and followed as they were carried from the car to their pen. Terrified by the upheaval in its young life, one piglet panicked in his new surroundings and squeezed through a small opening in the fence. He fled squealing into the nearby woods. Annie immediately disappeared into the brush after him. After a few seconds the piglet reappeared, guided by Annie toward the owner, who was able to pounce on the piglet and deliver him safely back into his pen.

Shiloh's family got a pet rabbit who became very fond of the dog. Her favorite place to sleep was by his side. The rabbit was bred and shortly before her babies were due she began to build a nest. The naked newborns were delivered into a nest lined not only with their mother's fur, but also with the downy undercoat of Shiloh, who patiently allowed his small friend to pluck him.

A cat which had been mistreated and maimed was adopted by Ad Lib's owners. The animal was terrified of humans but he formed an early attachment to the Newf. The dog's patience and gentleness finally taught the cat that his world was no longer threatening and he became a well-adjusted member of the family. He loved to play with the dogs, especially the puppies. He had his own door into the barn which was protected by a small fence, low enough for him to jump over but high enough to keep out the puppies. This afforded a refuge when he wanted relief from them.

The cat was fifteen years old when Ad Lib's five-week-old puppies were first put into the yard for exercise and air. Despite his age, the cat welcomed the opportunity to play and stationed himself among the pups. Ad Lib had known the cat since her own puppyhood, but she was not at ease seeing him with her unweaned brood. She streaked across the yard, delicately hooked his flea collar with her canine teeth, gently carried him to his own yard, and deposited him behind his fence.

Banty was a Golden Bantam hen. She was semi-wild and was used to scratching for herself. So when her owners moved, and she could not be caught, she stayed on with the new owners, who had five adult Newfs. There was no problem with the adult dogs, but litters of puppies and a succession of young dogs, raised by the owners, took turns chasing her until they were trained to leave her alone. Then for a period of about four years, there were no puppies and no harassment. Little by little, Banty ventured closer to the dogs until she came to depend upon them for the companionship a hen normally finds within a flock. She picked up her seed on the patio among the dogs, she scrambled with them for a share of the salad greens tossed out to the dogs, and she would squat on the patio or picnic table to rest among them as if they were her flock.

Her peace was shattered when the owners bought three puppies. Again the victim of the chase, she became wary until the training of the puppies was completed. Her dependence upon the dogs' company was so strong that she took up her old position among them at the earliest opportunity. The puppies spent most of their time outdoors and were fed on the patio. Once Banty felt at ease with them a new opportunity presented itself. Slowly she began to approach the dog Bently at feeding time. Finding no threat, she was soon sharing his dinner. She appeared every evening at the pups' dinner time, until late fall when instinct forced her to go to roost with the early darkness, before the dogs were fed.

Yeti, an overweight bitch, was an escape artist. She seemed to have an understanding that she was not supposed to leave her run, because she freed herself only when no one was watching. Her owners would find her in the yard with the gate to her run closed and no holes in or under the fence.

One day when visitors were looking at a litter of puppies in an adjacent run, she apparently forgot herself in her desire to share some of the attention the puppies were getting. Owner and visitors watched with some astonishment as the bulky bitch slowly climbed the swaying wire fence and perched on top, waiting to steady herself for the five-foot drop into the puppy run. Climbing was the last skill the owners could have expected from this rotund bitch and it had never entered their minds that it was her method of escape.

Ebony, a yearling bitch, was absorbed by new wind chimes installed on a gusty day. But she was not quite at ease with their changing combination of movement and sound. She barked when they were first hung and continued to bark when she heard them throughout the day. Finally her owner led her to the chimes, reached up, and rattled them to assure the youngster they were harmless.

The next day was clear and calm so Ebony's owners were surprised to hear a loud clattering of the chimes. They looked through the window to see what was going on. There was Ebony on a lawn chair under the chimes, holding the wind paddle in her teeth and shaking it. She jumped down from the chair when she found herself being watched, but apparently was satisfied because she never troubled herself over the wind chimes again.

Teddy had an unusual way of communicating. If the car keys came out and he hoped to go along, if it was his dinnertime and his owners were not tending to business, or if he was uneasy with a situation, his owners would feel a warm paw hooked around one leg in an anxious, but firm, embrace.

He loved company and when he became senior dog in the household he was often allowed to be with the guests. Even non-dog lovers became enchanted when he would sit down beside them on the sofa with his bottom on the cushion and his forefeet kept properly on the floor.

One evening Teddy was sitting next to a guest who was describing an unhappy family situation. He seemed to sense her distress, and breaking his own rule of "feet on the floor," he lay over and put his head in her lap. His comforting gesture was received gratefully.

Ben, a Newfoundland who lived in Montana, became a self-appointed ranch hand. He insisted on helping whenever his owner carried anything and delivered the items to house or barn. When the snow was too deep for the truck, Ben was hitched to a sled to haul wood to the house or hay to the horses. As a puppy, Ben caught and led back a horse which had broken away from its owners. After that Ben helped regularly in leading the horses.

Ethan and Golly were among several generations of Newfs trained as pack dogs. They carried their own food and water and light gear, rarely totaling as much as twenty pounds. The Newfs were accepted as partners who, through their special sensitivities, could add to the experience of wilderness travel and, to some extent, could serve as protection.

Both dogs became very useful at finding the trail. Although they had been trained in wilderness manners and safety, they required no training in trail finding. It was under circumstances of need that each dog first demonstrated this ability.

Their owner was used to hiking off trail or following animal paths which crisscrossed one another. On the return trip he sometimes would be uncertain as to which trail would lead back. One late afternoon in winter he found himself in such a situation. The remaining daylight did not allow time for trial and error and although equipped, he was not anxious to spend an unplanned night in the woods.

He said to his dog, "Golly, find the trail," and motioned for the dog to go ahead. Golly, who had been trained to walk behind, went ahead a few steps on one of the paths. Then he paused, looked over his shoulder, and waited for his partner to take the lead. The trail he had selected led back to the car.

Ethan, who came several generations after Golly, demonstrated his ability under similar circumstances. He not only could find the way back, but also could find the way to a certain destination in situations where a trail had long been abandoned and visual clues were insufficient for a human to follow.

It is not remarkable that the dogs, with their acute senses

of smell, could find the right trails. What is remarkable is the Newfoundland's ability to understand a need and respond appropriately to it.

Sugar's understanding of a need, combined with typical Newfoundland pleasure in fetching and carrying, caused her to be assigned a useful daily task.

Some Newfs will find objects to carry around the house or yard—sticks, bones, or a favorite toy. Sugar liked to be given items to carry or fetch for a purpose. She and her companion Newf, Carrie, were fed outside. One day at feeding time their owner remembered that she had been in a hurry and had not picked up the dogs' dishes after their previous meal.

On impulse she told Sugar to fetch the bowls. The dog understood and promptly retrieved a bowl and delivered it to her owner. Sent for the second bowl, she did the same thing. From that time on Sugar brought in the bowls each day. Clever as she was, however, she could not count, so when the Newf family increased from two to four, Sugar enthusiastically continued to go back for bowls until she was told, "That's all, Sug."

Humans are familiar with instinctive canine traits, such as tail wagging, scent marking, and courting behavior, because they can see their dogs function on a day-to-day basis. Occasionally, it is possible to catch a glimpse of a different form of behavior which seems hauntingly primitive and unfamiliar.

It is suggested in Newfoundland literature that native dogs, which were possible ancestors of the Newf, were used by the Indians for fishing. The dogs supposedly were trained to catch fish and to stack them on shore.

It is also said that Newfs on the island of Newfoundland were turned loose during the winter when their labor was not needed. Left to fend for themselves, they survived at least partially by eating the cambium layer of trees for nourishment.

These are fascinating possibilities, considering that Newfs can and will catch fish and that Newfs have a propensity for eating wood. Many Newfs will chew on a stick with as much enthusiasm as on a bone. They eat wood and woody shrubs. Two young dogs devoured eight rosebushes, thorns and all, over a period of just a few days.

A puzzling episode took place one day when Golly went with his owners to a remote mountain lake. It was a small body of water, very shallow and totally clear. Golly went into the water as expected, but it was not deep enough for him to swim. He became preoccupied in ducking for pieces of wood which he could see at the bottom of the lake. After picking up a piece of wood, he waded to shore and deposited it before going back for another stick. He persisted at this for some time, oblivious to anything else. Finally, the wood he chose to pick up happened to be the branch of a tree which had toppled into the water. He ducked repeatedly, intent upon freeing the wood without realizing his impossible task.

Finally his owners called him to leave. They sensed something primordial in the dog's behavior while he was occupied in the lake. It was as if a switch had been turned on in his mind and he had temporarily reverted to a more primitive state.

The events of the afternoon suggested the possibility that something had triggered a set of ancient instincts, confused by domestication, and translated into non-productive behavior. Perhaps they were the same instincts, still integrated in earlier times, which allowed the Newfoundlands turned loose on the island to survive.

American and Canadian Ch. Seamount Sally Forth, bred and owned by Alan and Jo Ann Riley, carries a sign at a street corner rally to help get the vote out for a school levy election.

Captain Benjamin's Portage, bred and owned by Ruth Burns, helps on the ranch.

Heroic Newfoundlands Honored

by Joyce Hieber

(The deeds of two Newfoundlands honored by the Newfoundland Club of America as reported in the *Newf Tide*, summer 1983. Each dog was awarded the Heroic Newfoundland Award at the 1983 National Specialty banquet. Reprinted by permission of *Newf Tide*.)

This year, for the first time in several years, two Newfoundlands were honored at the National Specialty banquet on May 28. Both were presented the Heroic Newfoundland Award for their deeds recounted below.

The first, a bronze male named Kodiak, is owned by Kathie Cullen of Glendale, California. Kathie sent this account of Kodiak's deed.

Late last fall, Kodiak and Kathie were enjoying a quiet evening at home when Kathie remembered she had not put any more beef melts on to cook for Kodiak's dinner. She prepared them, putting them on the gas stove to cook over a low flame. Kodiak was tired and too warm in the house so she put him outside and finished getting ready for bed.

Kathie said she was very tired, it was late and the meat was taking forever to cook. So she turned the flame lower and went to lie down, returning to check on them in about 15 minutes. Cooking so late at night—it was close to midnight by now—was not her normal practice but she was in a hurry to be done. She went back to lie down, thinking she'd get up in a few minutes to turn off the flame.

The next thing Kathie remembered was the sound of pounding on her front door. Her sleep was deep and she had great difficulty in awakening. Dimly she knew it must be Kodiak wanting back inside but the dog had never been so insistent. She could hear the screen door being shredded by his nails. Angrily, Kathie finally sat up, turned on the light, and discovered the room was filled with smoke. The clock read 5:00 AM—the beef melts had been on the stove all night!

Dashing to the kitchen, Kathie found the pot on the stove practically empty. She turned off the flame and ran to the front door where Kodiak met her whining. Together they went into the yard where the dog covered her with wet sloppy licks. He continued to whine and lick her, crowding close and staying between her and the house. When she attempted to return to the house, Kodiak grabbed her hand, trying to pull her back into the yard. Finally, together, they entered the house so Kathie could open windows.

In Kathie Cullen's own words, "Kodiak had no reason to want in the house, he was completely safe outside; but yet this noble Newf knew that there was something wrong and he wanted me out of that house."

The second recipient, a black female named Dirigo's Magnificent Villa, CD, is owned by Lynda Veit of Villas, New Jersey.

Riptide's Brown Kodiak Bear, W.D., and owner Kathie J. Cullen.

On February 11, during the Blizzard of 1983, at about 3:45 P.M. an 11-year-old girl named Andrea Anderson was driven by 50–60 mph winds into a deep snowdrift just 40 feet from her home, and within 15 feet of the Delaware Bay. Futilely she tried to free herself. When wind-driven snow and sand prevented her from even opening her eyes, she became frightened and began screaming for help.

Villa, the Newfoundland, was apparently the only living creature to hear Andrea's screams. For the first time in her life, Villa scaled the five-foot fence enclosing her run. She covered the 80 feet separating her from the child and began licking Andrea's face. Villa circled, clearing the snow and allowed Andrea to grab hold of her coat, then pulled her from the drift. She plowed the way back to Andrea's home where Mrs. Bea Anderson, Andrea's mother, saw the child holding onto the dog's neck outside their front door. When Andrea was safe inside, Villa returned home and scratched on the front door. Mrs. Anderson's phone call to Lynda solved the mystery of how Villa got out of her run, and why she had left it.

In Lynda's words, "Though chances are great that Andrea would have survived the frightening experience, Villa reinforced the fact that Newfoundland dogs have that innate gift of lifesaving."

How lucky we all are to be owned by Newfoundlands.

Andrea, Lynda Veit, and Villa.

A four-month-old Briny Deep puppy, bred by Claire Ives, looks out seriously upon the world.

Choosing a Newfoundland

The purchase of a puppy represents a long-term investment of time and money and should be approached with deliberation. You will need to consider: Do you want a pet and companion, a protector, a show dog? Do you want to participate in water or obedience competitions? Do you want a male or a female? Do you want a puppy or an older dog? You may not know the answers to these questions until you begin looking for a dog. Attending dog shows and observing Water Tests, visiting kennels, and talking to breeders and fanciers will help you make these decisions.

Most buyers want a Newf for several purposes, which can be satisfied by any well-bred healthy puppy that looks and acts like a Newf. The buyer with showing or breeding in mind has a more difficult task in finding the right puppy. Showing and breeding require a considerable commitment of time and money, as well as a long learning process. A firm decision whether to show and/or breed should be made before the search for a puppy or dog begins.

You may have a strong preference for one sex over the other. If this is not the case, either sex should be equally satisfying. Females (referred to as bitches) tend to be a bit more dependent, and males (referred to as dogs), more exploratory. Both are very much oriented toward people and rarely show extreme favoritism for a single person in the family. On the whole, dogs are larger than bitches and have proportionately larger heads. The drawbacks of coming into season traditionally have made bitches less desirable than dogs as pets. The availability of safe, inexpensive spaying has eliminated that problem.

Most people seem to prefer starting with a puppy. The joys of raising a puppy usually outweigh the disadvantages. But under some circumstances, a grown Newf should be considered. A working family, gone all day, will find that a typical mature adult dog will be more content when left alone than will an active puppy, and the adult dog will require less training to live in a household. Older or handicapped individuals will find a mature adult dog to be calmer and more easily managed than a puppy. Families with very young children may find it easier to adopt an older dog that does not require the watchful tending required by puppies.

Some young adult Newfs are quite exuberant, but by two years of age most are typical of the breed—calm, placid, and gentle.

Most Newfs adapt easily to a loving new family, and unless a dog has established some undesirable habits which cannot be managed, the adoption will be a success. The new owner should be advised of any health or behavior problems the dog may have in order to be prepared to cope with them. Some of the happiest adoptions have been with "problem dogs" nursed back to physical or emotional health by loving owners. But it is an injustice to all concerned unless this kind of task is taken on with great deliberation. It may be possible to take an adult dog on a trial basis. Agreements regarding the return of a dog should be made in writing and signed by both parties.

Most Newfs are highly trainable and can succeed in various training activities such as obedience, tracking, Water Tests, carting, and backpacking. Some breeders are especially interested in these activities, encouraging their puppy buyers to participate and offering assistance and advice.

Any large dog with a deep bark offers protection for its family simply by its presence. This is the basic kind of protection most Newf owners expect from their dogs. It is a mistake, however, to train a Newf as a guard dog, and it is surely an injustice to the dog. This breed is naturally trusting and gentle. It would require a traumatic change in the dog's basic character to turn it into a true guard dog.

When you are in the process of deciding what qualities you want in a Newfoundland, you will also be in the process of choosing a breeder from whom to purchase your dog, and, eventually, choosing that puppy or dog.

It is not always possible to visit a number of kennels. There are areas of the country where Newfs are indeed rare. In this case the best alternative would be to write to a number of breeders and to telephone those whose responses interest you most.

Dog shows are an excellent place to learn about the breed and to talk to breeders and fanciers. It is best to wait until after the Newfoundlands have been judged, however. Before the judging, most exhibitors are preoccupied with getting ready to show their dogs. At any show there may be dogs representing a number of kennels, both from local and other areas. Breeders and fanciers with a wide range of experience will be able to answer questions about Newfs and to offer information on available puppies.

Before visiting a kennel, call to make an appointment. Breeding dogs of good quality is a hobby rather than a business and kennels usually are an adjunct of the breeder's home. There generally are no regular business hours at a breeding kennel and the prospective buyer is a guest, rather than a customer who comes at his own convenience.

Do not judge a kennel by the elegance of its facilities. Look instead to see whether there is adequate space for the dogs, appropriate shelter, security, fresh water, and general cleanliness. A few fresh stools are not an indication of carelessness, but old stools and odor indicate the dogs may not be well cared for. Above all, watch the dogs. Even if they are not immaculately groomed, they should be glossy-coated, bright-eyed, curious, energetic, and responsive.

If there is a litter of puppies, their dam may be the least appealing of all the dogs. Raising a litter is stressful and the dam may appear thin and out of coat. Do not judge the rest of the kennel on her less-than-usually-attractive appearance.

Pet puppies may be purchased from one who simply has bred his or her pet dog to another pet. However, there is a greater risk of dissatisfaction in this situation than in getting a pet from a reputable breeder. "Pet breeders" rarely know the breed other than from experience with their own dogs. They do not know bloodlines, are unaware of genetic problems, may not know how to care properly for the dam and her puppies, cannot offer advice on raising puppies, and do not have a list of resources on health, training, and Newf activities. They may not know the protocol of selling puppies, such as sales agreements and guarantees, nor the AKC rules regarding registration. They do not keep up on canine literature concerning feeding, health, and immunization. They may have bred a litter thinking of earning a profit, and found the usual high costs overwhelming. Puppy diet, immunization, and health care may be sacrificed to make ends meet. Finally, the puppies may turn out neither to look nor to act like typical Newfoundlands.

Buying a puppy from a pet shop holds the same hazards. But, in addition, the pet shop puppy will have been exposed to many other dogs and puppies at a time when its immune status is questionable. It will have been denied exercise and socialization while confined awaiting sale.

This is not to suggest that Newfs should be purchased only from large breeding kennels. Every breeder has to start small. A single-bitch owner who has become involved in learning about the breed, shows the bitch, and belongs to a regional and/or the national Newfoundland club, may produce excellent puppies. It is a breeder's commitment to the breed which determines the quality of the kennel. Many excellent Newfs are the products of beginning breeders.

No breeder can guarantee anything about a puppy except that its pedigree is accurate and that its health is satisfactory at the time of sale. The puppy's genes and environment will determine its future health, temperament, intelligence, and appearance. If you are told that a puppy is a certain show winner, take heed. At best, a puppy can be described only as a show *prospect*. Even a gorgeous puppy with an impeccable pedigree may develop faults which will make it unsuitable as a show competitor.

Reputable breeders often have waiting lists for their puppies and have buyers returning for additional purchases. They do not charge significantly higher or lower prices than other breeders. They do not try to make a specific dog or puppy seem more valuable because of a rare characteristic. On the whole, rare characteristics are undesirable because they do not conform to the breed Standard.

Many breeders will agree to replace, or to refund money for, a puppy that dies or is unable to function as a pet because of genetic or congenital defects.

If one has confidence in the breeder, choosing the right pet from a litter is a matter of appeal. A breeder normally grades the puppies for show potential. Those considered to be show or breeding prospects may command a higher price or be sold only to buyers willing to show them. If there is a waiting list for the litter, those ordering show or breeding prospects will be offered first choice of puppies.

Pet buyers may not be able to discern a difference between the pet and show prospects, particularly in a uniform litter. Pet puppies will have been raised with the same care and concern for health and development as the show prospects.

If the litter is close enough to visit one or more times before a choice is made, the buyer has an opportunity to determine more about the puppies. A normally energetic pup may appear timid or restrained on the first visit, and a normally quiet pup may exhibit unusually high spirits. If you have a preference for either extreme, you should ask the breeder to confirm your assessment of a particular puppy.

Traits to avoid are timidity or shyness. A shy, fearful adult dog has an unreliable temperament and is to be avoided, even over an aggressive dog whose normal responses are a known factor. Fortunately timidity, shyness, and aggressiveness are all very rare characteristics in Newfoundlands.

Novice buyers of show prospects are well advised to ask the breeder to help in selecting a puppy. The buyer who has made an effort to learn about the breed and has approached the purchase of a puppy with care and deliberation will have chosen that breeder with good reason. It is appropriate to trust that person's judgment as to the best possible puppy to select. If one or more pups are of comparable quality, the breeder will explain the strengths and weaknesses of each. At that point the buyer will need to decide which factors are most important, or simply which puppy is most appealing.

Breeding prospects are chosen with equal care. Anyone interested in breeding obviously would start with a puppy bitch. Many breeders require that buyers of pet bitches sign an agreement to have them spayed. The same breeders selling breeding prospects may require certain commitments on the part of a first-time Newf buyer. Such commitments could include membership in a Newfoundland club, showing the bitch, allowing the breeder to choose a stud for a first mating, and requiring that the bitch be assessed as an adult for her merits as a brood bitch. The intent of such agreements is to protect the breed from indiscriminate breeding by unknowledgeable individuals who are unconcerned for the future of the breed.

Males generally are not purchased for breeding purposes,

although some people buy dogs with that intent. Unless a dog is outstanding in quality, he will not be sought out as a stud dog. While it is appropriate to "advertise," in dog show catalogs and other dog periodicals, that a stud dog is available, it is not considered proper protocol in the dog world to ask the owner of a bitch to breed the bitch to one's dog.

Occasionally someone will plan to buy a puppy dog and a puppy bitch, intending to breed them at maturity. This is a mistake. The puppies may mature to be unsuitable mates. In breeding, one attempts to compensate, in one mate, for the faults of the other. Owning a male and a female creates a great temptation to breed them, despite the fact that such a mating may enhance certain faults. In addition, one or both dogs may not be of breeding quality. If one wishes to begin with two puppies, it is far better to buy two bitches than to buy a male and a female.

If a bitch is of good quality, one has a wide range of choices for stud dogs. Finding the right stud will enable the bitch to produce puppies as good as or better than herself. This is what breeding is all about. It is also far less expensive and less troublesome to pay an occasional stud fee than to buy and maintain a male. It is almost intolerable to keep a male in the same kennel with a bitch in season, unless one has special facilities. Even then the male dog and the owners are put to considerable stress.

Following is a list of papers which the breeder should provide the buyer at the time of sale:

1. A properly completed and signed, individual AKC registration slip, or an agreement signed by buyer and seller as to when, and under what circumstances, the slip will be provided. The AKC requires that the registration slip be given with the puppy unless there is an agreement in writing to the contrary. Any contingencies, upon which provision of the individual registration slip are based, should be specifically and clearly stated.

2. A pedigree of three or more generations.

3. A sales agreement signed by buyer and seller describing the puppy, its sex, color and markings, litter number, date whelped, names and AKC registration numbers of sire and dam, agreements regarding guarantees, breeding or showing rights or obligations, spaying or neutering agreements, amount paid and installment payment agreements, and any other agreements regarding the puppy.

4. Care and feeding instructions.

5. An immunization and worming history and schedule.

6. A veterinary certificate of health.

A well-bred puppy is the product of considerable investment on the part of the breeder. Expertise based upon years of study and experience, a sizeable financial outlay, and plain hard work are represented in each puppy. It is understandable that the breeder is as concerned with the placement of his or her puppies as the buyer is in choosing well. One of life's happiest moments is when a puppy or dog is turned over to its new owner after frank questioning and discussion has satisfied both buyer and breeder that each has made a good choice.

Two Halirock puppies "puzzling" over a wooden Newfoundland puzzle.

A litter of black and Landseer puppies at Seaward Kennels.

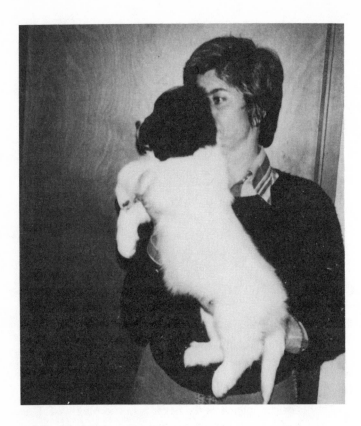

An eight-week-old Steamboat puppy being held with chest and rear supported.

Adult Newf introducing a puppy to water.

The Newfoundland Puppy

Prepare for your Newfoundland before he arrives. The most basic considerations are management strategies. Decide, in advance, in what parts of the house the dog will be allowed, where he will sleep, who will be responsible for housebreaking, feeding, and cleanup, where he will stay when no one is at home, and how he will be protected from hazards inside and out.

Some supplies and equipment should be purchased in advance. These will include items such as utensils for food and water and any equipment indicated by your management plan, such as a baby gate, crate, doghouse, and fencing.

Bringing home a new puppy is the climax of what may have been months of searching and planning. It is a moment of joy, excitement, and fulfillment. It is also a time of stress for puppy and owners. The normal order of a household becomes disrupted by the needs of a small demanding creature who must adapt to a new and bewildering situation. During the day, attention from his new owners distracts the new puppy from an awareness of the loss of familiar surroundings and the comfort of siblings. But for the first night, and sometimes for several nights, puppy and owner suffer from the trauma of the changes in lifestyle. A ticking wind-up alarm clock and a soft pillow or stuffed toy may help substitute for the litter mates the puppy is used to snuggling up to at night. Allowing the puppy to sleep in the same room as a human companion helps the puppy to feel less alone. An owner determined to housebreak a pup as quickly as possible can set an alarm to go off two or three times during the night and take the pup out to eliminate, encouraging the puppy's natural tendency to keep his sleeping quarters clean. A puppy that becomes acclimated to his new home by sleeping in the bedroom can be moved later to some other sleeping area preferred by the owner.

If the owner prefers that the pup begin his new life in a designated sleeping area, the number of sleepless nights to be expected will vary from pup to pup. A puppy will adapt to such an area more readily at night if he spends some time there during the day learning to be alone. He should be provided with safe chew toys for amusement and security.

A portable dog crate or kennel makes an ideal "bedroom" for a puppy. Once acclimated to a crate, the puppy will consider it his own private retreat and security area. The puppy can be kept there when the owner is away from home, when guests are present, or any time the family is too busy to keep an eye on him. He will tend not to foul this confined area, and will learn bladder and bowel control.

Solid-wall crates are made of fiberglass, aluminum, or wood. These have a ventilating "door" and "windows." Wire crates are made of heavy gauge, rigid wire and are completely ventilated. Although not inexpensive, a crate is an investment which will last the lifetimes of several dogs. It is advisable to buy one for a puppy which will continue to serve him as an adult. A two by three by four foot crate will accommodate the largest Newf. A crate also increases the dog's safety in a truck or station wagon, and when traveling it offers a secure and familiar area of confinement in motels and campgrounds. All but wire crates are accepted by airlines for shipping dogs.

Training a dog or puppy to accept a crate takes time and patience. It may take several days of feeding, offering treats, and playing with the puppy while he is in the crate with the door open before he is ready to spend a very short time in it with the door closed. He needs to understand from the beginning that being put in the crate does not mean he will be there forever. He also needs to associate the crate with pleasurable experiences.

Sleeping areas, as well as all other areas in which the pup will be allowed, must be made safe for him. Garages, laundry rooms, and kitchens all have their share of toxic materials which must be placed out of reach. Other hazards include small objects which might be swallowed, sharp or brittle objects which might be chewed, sharp projections, toxic plants, heavy objects which a pup might pull down upon himself, and open stairwells. Another danger is electric cords, which are appealing to puppies. There is usually no second chance for learning the hazard of an electric cord once a pup bites into one.

"Safe toys" are a worthwhile investment in many respects. They provide amusement and satisfy a puppy's need to chew, but are also useful for socialization and training. Safe toys for puppies and adult dogs include hard English rubber toys and balls, knotted socks, old tennis shoes and leather gloves, nylon bones, and rawhide chew toys. Unsafe toys include soft or hollow rubber balls and toys, golf balls, toys with bells or squeakers, brittle plastic objects, and most bones. Chicken and rib bones, which can splinter, can be lethal.

When a puppy picks up or chews on a forbidden object, tell him "No" in a loud voice and substitute a safe toy for the object. Most Newfs quickly learn what they may and may not play with.

Newfs are natural retrievers and puppies love to chase balls, sticks, and toys. This activity gives puppy and owner

A Newf owned by Little Bear Kennels.

Ch. Shipshape's Cutty Sark shown winning the class for six-month to nine-month-old puppies at the 1967 National Specialty. "Scotty," owned by Shipshape Kennels, was a popular stud dog of the 1970s.

a chance to play and can be a training session at the same time. If a puppy does not return a retrieved object, squat down and encourage him to come. Most dogs that refuse to come when called will respond when the caller squats, if they are rewarded with praise for coming. Never punish a dog when he comes to you. If he must be corrected for failure to come when called, go to him and correct him. If you have waited for him to come to you, praise him, regardless of how long it has taken.

When the puppy returns a retrieved item, tell him to "Give," and take the item. If he refuses to give it up, place one hand over his muzzle and squeeze between the jaws. It does not take much pressure to get the jaws to relax. Again say "Give" and praise the pup. Done repeatedly, the puppy will learn to bring to you anything he may be carrying, and to give it up.

It is natural for puppies to pursue things that move. In the nest, they begin as early as three to four weeks to bite feebly at each other's tails and legs. As they grow, puppies in a litter begin to play games of stalk and chase which end up with one pup tackling another, and both chewing and biting while struggling for a position on the top. Presumably, this is part of the inherent canine process of establishing the pack hierarchy, as well as practice for life as a predator in which skills of stalking, attacking, and killing are necessary for survival.

Young puppies will also mouth, chew, and bite at the moving parts of humans—feet, legs, and hands. Walking into a litter of five- or six-week-old puppies may require great dexterity in peeling puppies off your pants legs in order to take the next step forward.

Most pups have to be taught that mouthing and chewing on humans is not acceptable behavior. With some, it takes only a few smacks under the chin, accompanied by a sharp "No!" to teach them not to bite. Others require a more prolonged period of correction. This process takes concentrated consistency. It is easy to overlook the mouthings of a pup that has been biting, but mouthing and biting are parts of the same behavior pattern. Mouthing should be corrected in the same way as biting until the pup learns that neither is acceptable. Sometimes a puppy will mouth or bite until corrected, then begin to lick. This is a desirable response. Licking is subservient behavior and should be rewarded with suitable sounds or words of praise. Children and guests should be made aware that chewing, mouthing, and biting are not acceptable. If you do not want others correcting your puppy, remove him until he has learned not to do this.

Puppies, like children, will test to find out what limits have been set for them. Dams growl or snap at pups that have gone too far. Puppies use this same behavior to assert themselves. It is common for a pup to growl when a bone or food is taken away or when he is resisting something not to his liking. This is the time to exert dominance over the puppy. Never let a puppy growl at you or anyone else whose behavior the puppy should accept. (Some puppies develop a protective instinct at an early age. Growling might be appropriate under some circumstances, even for a puppy.) Immediate and firm correction is required, and should be repeated until the growling stops. A dog the size of a Newfoundland cannot be allowed to learn that he can threaten you or anyone accepted by you. You should not assume that your puppy will test his limits by growling, but you should not be alarmed if he does. This is not abnormal behavior nor a sign of poor temperament, even for a Newf.

If your puppy has never growled, it would be appropriate to set up a situation, while he is still small, to give him the opportunity to do so. Try to make the situation natural. For example, pick up his food dish while he is eating and move it to another spot, or take away a toy or a bone. Be businesslike and act as if you have a purpose—to put the bone away, for example. This will avoid any suggestion of teasing. If the puppy growls, correct him firmly. Repeat the provocations occasionally, and correct the pup if he growls, until he learns that growling is unacceptable.

Tug of war is a natural game for a puppy to play. The puppy should be the one to do the pulling so he will not be injured by his stronger human playmate. If he becomes too aggressive and excited, it is best to call a halt. In play activities between puppy and human, desirable habits and attitudes should be encouraged. Roughhousing with a puppy will not encourage him to be gentle. Children tend to play with puppies as they play with their friends, and should be taught to avoid rough play with puppies.

Decide on the limits you will set for your puppy and be consistent in enforcing them. Lack of consistency will confuse the puppy and make training difficult for him and for you.

Housebreaking

Newfoundlands are not difficult to housebreak if the process is approached with consistency and concentration. It pays to devote a week or two toward getting the puppy trained, avoiding a long, drawn-out process which is hard on everyone.

There are three basic principles in housebreaking: one, confine the puppy to a single room where he can be monitored constantly; two, take him outside at the appropriate times; and, three, confine him to a small area such as a crate or laundry room when he cannot be watched.

When the puppy is with you, watch for him to sniff the floor while moving at increased speed. Take him outside before he eliminates on the floor. If he does have an accident, say "No!" sharply, pick him up, and take him outside. Wait until he eliminates again, praise him, and take him back inside.

Puppies routinely should be taken out after eating, after playing, and after taking a nap. Under nine or ten weeks

Three-week-old puppy from Sue Jones's Mooncusser Kennels.

Newfoundlands are self-appointed lifeguards when children are in or near the water. Joan Foster and her children with one of their Newfs.

of age, a pup reasonably could be taken out every half hour while he is awake. Taking him to the same place outside each time will help him learn what he is to do at that spot.

Never scold or punish a pup for an error you have not witnessed. He simply will not understand why he is being chastised. Consider the error your own for not watching him closely. Punishment and harsh scolding are not appropriate to the housebreaking process in any situation. Until a puppy is old enough to have control of his bladder and bowels, and until he has had sufficient training to understand what to do when he needs relief, he will do what nature demands. Between ten and twelve weeks puppies become capable of better control, with the frequency of urination reduced. Many will stay dry and clean all night if confined to a small area, and most will have few accidents during the day if they have had consistent training for a week or two.

Physical punishment should be necessary only long enough to teach an understanding of the word "No." It is essential that a puppy learn this word early in his training, both for his own safety and for the well-being of the owner and his or her property. "No" can be accompanied by a smack under the lower jaw or by grasping the loose skin on the chest and shaking the pup. Obviously the size and age of the puppy should be considered in determining the amount of force to use. Once the puppy responds to "No," physical punishment should not be necessary unless the command is disregarded. The one exception in accompanying "No" with punishment is in housebreaking.

An old spatula works well for picking up stools in the house. Urine on carpets should be soaked up first. Rubbing tends to spread and soak it further into the fibers. An excellent odor killer is a solution of twenty-five percent white vinegar to seventy-five percent water. After soaking up as much urine as possible, spray with the vinegar solution and rub in well. This solution is safe for most fibers but should first be tested on a small area before being used on a regular basis.

Feeding

An experienced breeder will provide a diet and feeding schedule when a puppy is delivered to his new owners. From eight weeks to six months, puppies usually are fed three times a day. The owner's schedule may require a change in the times of day when the pup is fed. He will adjust to the change, but consistency is important. Mammals have a sense of time and a puppy needs the security of being fed when his "clock" tells him it is time.

It is best not to alter a pup's diet immediately. Ask, before you take your puppy home, what he is eating, including the specific brand of food. Stock it ahead of time. If you have reason to change the diet, do so gradually by mixing in the new food in increasing proportions over a few days' time.

Puppies are most expensive to feed during the year of rapid growth. A six-month-old pup probably will eat more than a two-year-old dog. Whatever the age, feed only top-quality brands of puppy or dog food.

Between eight weeks and about six months, a Newfoundland pup will gain from three to five pounds per week. It is helpful to weigh the pup weekly in order to know when to increase his ration. If he is gaining less than three pounds per week it is probably time to increase the amount at each feeding by one-half cup. Do not let a puppy gain four or five pounds per week on a regular basis. It is generally acknowledged that overfeeding is more dangerous than underfeeding.

Self-feeding, with dry food available at all times, was once a widely accepted practice based on the theory that dogs will regulate their own intakes. This feeding method is held less favorably today, especially for growing puppies. There are specific orthopedic diseases thought to be associated with overeating, and other diseases which may be exacerbated by it. Greedy or bored puppies are particularly at risk. They will eat all they can hold. The owner should be aware that the recommended feeding amounts on puppy and dog food packages are often far more than the puppy will need to gain three pounds a week.

As for human diet, recommendations for canine diet have been undergoing changes. At one time giant breeds were fed a variety of supplements. Those owners who still supplement have had success with such diets and continue to supplement with good reason. However, it has become more common to depend upon a good brand of puppy food with few or no supplements.

Some puppies seem to be hungry all of the time, creating the temptation to feed more than is necessary for proper health. There is also the temptation among first-time owners to get their "big" dogs as big as possible. Size is determined by genes, and unless a pup suffers from malnutrition, he will grow to his full potential on a moderate diet.

Overnutrition and overweight are separate conditions, though they may be found in combination. Overweight in adult dogs is harmful in the same way it is in humans. Overweight and overnutrition in a puppy can be devastating. Even if a pup does not develop a disease associated with overnutrition, additional weight on his fast-growing joints and ligaments can affect his development, causing permanent damage. If in doubt about your puppy's weight and development, consult your veterinarian.

Special utensils are not needed for food and water, but many owners prefer those made of stainless steel for durability and easy cleaning.

Fresh water should be available indoors and out for dogs that spend time both places. A device which attaches to a hose or faucet permits a dog to drink at will without the need of a bucket or bowl. If a bucket is to be used for an outside water dish, stainless steel is ideal. A galvanized bucket with a rough surface is difficult to clean. Enamel is easy to clean, but it chips readily. Plastic is satisfactory for adult dogs, but puppies often play with empty buckets and can destroy plastic containers quickly.

Newfs are untidy drinkers. Indoors, a water bowl or bucket may be placed in a newspaper-lined kitty litter tray or in a plastic dishpan. The paper will absorb splashes and spills and can be replaced as needed.

Exercise and Conditioning

There are a few cautions to be considered in providing exercise. Some joggers engaged in fitness programs like to include their dogs. Common sense dictates that a dog should not be expected to join a jogger who has worked himself up to a certain regimen, unless the dog has had a similar period of conditioning. In warm weather even a conditioned Newfoundland may not be able to exercise for his usual length of time because of his heavy coat and his inability to dissipate heat fast enough. A human dissipates heat over thousands of square inches of skin area. The dog's cooling system consists mainly of his mouth area through which he pants.

Walking, jogging, and hiking all improve lung, heart, and vascular capacity in humans, but sometimes take their toll on the joints and feet. The dog's joints and feet also are subject to injury. His footgear is what he is born with. Time is needed to toughen pads accustomed to lawn or carpet. Pads that have been toughened are still susceptible to cuts, bruises, and damage from hot pavements.

Time spent in jumping to catch balls and discs also should be increased gradually. Such activity involves the use of muscles, ligaments, and tendons not used in walking and running.

Fast-growing joints need special consideration with regard to exercise. Soft cartilage is more susceptible to injury than adult bone. Prolonged or stressful exercise and play should be avoided during the rapid growth period of the puppy's first year. Despite their size, giant breeds are more susceptible to joint injury than average-sized dogs during this period. Give your puppy a chance to grow up before including him in your hiking or jogging activities.

Children should not be allowed to play roughly or to pull, push, or press down on a puppy, nor to grab him by the legs. Try to avoid letting a pup leap from steps or furniture. Newf pups need not be "kept in cotton wool," but in play, in exercise, and when being handled, reasonable consideration must be given in order to avoid unnecessary stress on the joints.

To lift and carry a heavy puppy, slip one hand under the rib cage so the hand supports the ribs with one or two fingers between the front legs. Lift the puppy so he is standing on the hind legs, then slip the other hand between the hind legs and lift. This method allows you to support the puppy without lifting him by the legs.

Health Care and Safety

An eight-week-old puppy should have had at least one immunization, including vaccines for distemper, leptospirosis, hepatitis, tracheobronchitis, and canine parvovirus If the breeder does not suggest a vaccination schedule, ask your vet when the next shot should be given. Puppies may be vaccinated from three to five times by the age of sixteen weeks.

Puppy shots are no different from annual boosters given to adult dogs. Puppy shots are given at more frequent interludes, not because increased amounts of vaccine are needed, but because puppies receive temporary immunity from the dam's colostrum (the milk secreted for a few days after whelping). The effectiveness of early shots may be blocked by this immunity. The curve of maternal immunity drops off as the puppy ages. By sixteen weeks a high percentage of puppies will have lost this immunity and will benefit from the effects of vaccines.

During the period between his first and final puppy shots, the puppy should not be exposed to dogs of unknown immune status. While it is not an ideal situation to keep a dog strictly confined to the owner's property, there is some risk involved in taking a young puppy to public places where other dogs have been. Canines gravitate to the scent of urine and feces. These are the most common transmitters of infectious canine diseases.

An eight-week-old puppy will have been checked for roundworms two or three times. Follow the breeder's recommendations for follow-up stool checks, or consult with your vet. If your puppy is from an area of the country where heartworm is a threat, the breeder should advise you as to the preventive medication the puppy has had. If you live in an area where heartworm infestation occurs, consult with your vet for a program of prevention.

During the flea season puppies and dogs need to be powdered, sprayed, or dipped frequently in order to keep fleas under control. Besides creating considerable discomfort, fleas transmit tapeworm and cause skin and coat problems. On young puppies it is best to use a product made specifically for that age dog. Flea collars are ineffective on large, heavily coated breeds.

A dog collar is a necessity from the time a new puppy is brought home. It provides a means of restraining and guiding the puppy and carries the license and identification tag. Collars on growing puppies need to be checked often to make certain they are not too tight. A Newf puppy will outgrow three or four collars by adulthood.

Training collars or slip collars are for use only when a dog is on a lead. They should never be left on a dog after the lead is removed. The dog's regular collar should be the buckle-on type made of flat or rolled leather.

When buying a lead for a puppy it is most economical to choose one which will last throughout his life. A four-to six-foot latigo lead is extremely durable. It should be three-quarters of an inch to one inch wide. Latigo is more supple than leather and is comfortable in the hands. It does not deteriorate from being soaked. Chain, nylon grosgrain, and cord leads are less expensive but are very hard on the hands when it is necessary to control a huge dog.

If you plan to train your dog for obedience, choose a six-foot length of lead, which is the length required in most obedience classes. There is an advantage to this length for general use as well. The extra length allows the dog to be tied to a picnic table, tree, or car bumper in public places.

Some puppies will accept a lead immediately and will trot along as if they had been perfectly trained. Some will become quite upset and fight the restraint. To prevent this possibility, put the collar on the pup, then attach the lead to it and let him drag the lead around the house. When the pup is accustomed to it, take him outside, pick up the end of the lead, and follow wherever he goes, putting little or no tension on the lead.

Gradually some tension may be applied. When the pup is comfortable with this, encourage him to change direction by talking in a pleasant voice while giving a quick tug on the lead.

While the pup is getting used to the lead, do not pull on it, because this will encourage him to resist. With quick tugs, use your voice to persuade him to go your way, giving lots of praise when he does so.

Once the puppy is willing to walk along with you, move briskly and change direction frequently. This will train him to watch where you are going in order to avoid the quick tugs he gets when taken by a surprise change of direction. The long-term benefit from a small effort in puppy training will be a grown dog that walks beside you without pulling and straining on the lead.

Ch. Indigo's Fritzacker, 1970 NCA National Specialty Best-of-Breed winner (bred and owned by Pauline and Myron O'Neil), with a young puppy.

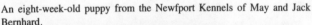

An eight-week-old puppy from the Newfport Kennels of May and Jack Bernhard.

A three-month-old Halirock puppy relaxes on the deck.

Ch.Pouch Cove Gref of Newton Ark, bred by Peggy Helming and Janet Levine, and owned by Julie Heyward, shows the poise of a veteran show dog. Gref is a multi-Group-placing Newf, well known through his champion progeny as a dominant sire.

Ch. Koki De Nashau-Auke, bred and owned by Jane and Ron Thibault, posing for his picture in the "four square" show stance. Koki won both Veteran and Stud-Dog Classes at the 1976 NCA National Specialty.

Care for the Adult Newfoundland

The Newfoundland requires the same basic care as any dog: food, water, shelter, physical protection, and medical care. In addition, long-coated breeds such as the Newfoundland require special grooming care.

Diet

The most practical diet for a large breed adult dog is a good quality dry commercial product. Bargain brands are no bargain if they fail to meet the dog's nutritional needs. Unless a dog has been spoiled by canned foods or table scraps he will find most commercial dry rations palatable. These rations are balanced and normally can make up the dog's total diet.

Adult Newfoundlands should be fed twice a day. If this is impractical, once-a-day feeding is acceptable. The dog should be given the opportunity to eliminate after feeding, but exercise should be delayed for an hour or more after eating.

Large, deep-chested breeds are susceptible to bloat, a potentially fatal phenomenon. The cause is unknown, despite significant research. The medical term for bloat is Acute Gastric Dilatation. It is a syndrome typified by a swelling of the abdomen. In some cases, the stomach rotates (volvulus), cutting off its blood supply. But distention of the abdomen due to the buildup of gases, even without stomach rotation, causes pressure on the vital organs and eventually leads to shock, then death. Early symptoms may include salivating, heavy panting, and a distressed look. Once a dog has begun to bloat, there is no chance of mistaking the problem. Emergency care is of greatest urgency. In the absence of knowledge as to the cause or causes of bloat, it is felt that the precautions of feeding two smaller meals, rather than one large meal, and restricting exercise after feeding, are well advised. Bloat is a potentially fatal disease and dog owners should consult their veterinarians about further preventive measures.

A balanced dry ration may not be adequate for all Newfs in all situations. Stresses such as extremely cold weather, prolonged periods of physical activity, illness, parasitic infestation, pregnancy, growth, and old age may make the usual ration inadequate in quantity or quality. Some signs of inadequate nutrition are: harsh or dry coat, skin problems, reduced energy level, lack of appetite, increased appetite, excessive water intake, and coprophagia (stool eating).

A tendency to produce soft stools is not uncommon in the giant breeds. If a dog appears and acts healthy in all other respects, it is probably safe for the owner to experiment with different brands of dog food to try to firm up the stools, unless the dog is suffering from diarrhea. Soft stools indicate that food is passing through the digestive system too quickly and the dog may not be getting full nutrition from the food.

Since the signs of inadequate nutrition may also be symptoms of other problems, it is advisable to seek veterinary assistance. Even if nutrition is the problem, it is necessary to determine the specific deficiency in order to correct it. Random supplementation may only compound the problem.

There is little or no justification for giving dogs treats on a regular basis. This establishes hard-to-break habits, encourages begging, and adds unneeded calories. For good health and longevity Newfs should not be permitted to become overweight. First-time Newf owners often overfeed, considering overweight to be normal. Excess weight overtaxes the cardiovascular system and stresses the joints.

Shelter and Protection

Newfoundlands that are house dogs need no special shelter. Dogs kept outdoors, either permanently or occasionally, do need shelter from rain and direct sun. Cold is rarely a problem with this breed. Many Newfs choose to lie on a snowy deck or patio rather than in a dog house, even in zero-degree weather. But a shelter up off the ground and out of the wind is necessary for the time when the dog seeks protection from the cold. It should be noted that dogs kept outside in cold weather usually need additional calories to compensate for those burned in keeping warm.

Newfoundlands, like all pets, are dependent on the protection that only the owner can provide. Breeders often require that prospective puppy buyers have a fenced yard or run.

Unfortunately, if a single dog is expected to spend most of his time alone in a run, the possibilities for exercise are limited and boredom is inevitable. A run can be an ideal place to keep a dog when the owners are gone, especially if he can exercise in a fenced yard or spend time in the house when his owners are home. Newfs are often diggers, and this trait should be considered when fencing a run or yard, especially if a dog is left alone in these areas. Extending the fencing in a trench underground makes digging out difficult. A concrete base for a run eliminates the digging problem but stays wet from rain and urine. Four to six inches of pea gravel is preferable from a drainage and sanitation

Above, Ch. Tuckamore's Dutch of Pouch Cove, bred by Peggy and David Helming, and owned by Barbara Finch and Peggy Helming.

Above, American and Canadian Ch. Anestesia's Magic Marker, National Specialty Best-of-Breed winner, bred by Ed Suiezikas and owned by Dulcie Heuback.

Above, Ch. Shadybrook's Try for an Oscar, C.D., W.R.D., bred and owned by Jeri and Richard Krokum.

Below, Ch. Oprasus of the Good Shepherd, bred by Jane Hockstrasser and owned by Betty and Paul Ramey.

Above, Ch. Edenglen's Beau Geste, bred by Edenglen Kennels and owned by Fran and Bob Dibble.

Below, American and Canadian Ch. Topmast's Prairie Queen, bred by Margaret Willmott and owned by Mary and Bob Price.

48

standpoint. Both concrete and gravel can be sanitized and deodorized by occasional application of a thirty to one solution of water and chlorine bleach.

Dogs should not be chained. Chains or ropes can be hazards in themselves. In addition, the dog is at the mercy of any person or dog that might harass or harm him. The danger not only is physical, but emotional as well.

Under no circumstances should a dog be allowed to run loose. It is fair neither to the dog nor to neighbors or passersby. The dangers to the dog are obvious: motor vehicles, poisoned or contaminated food or water, and irate humans; or the possibility of theft or becoming lost.

Many devoted dog owners regularly take their dogs with them in the car. Most Newfs welcome the opportunity for a change of scenery. The best way to carry a dog in any vehicle is in a portable crate or kennel, which offers protection for both dog and human in case of an accident. However, today's compact cars will not accommodate a crate large enough for a Newf. Removable barriers, available through pet shops, act as a grille between the rear of a station wagon and the seats. In a sedan the dog should be trained to sit or lie down so as not to interfere with the driver. It is useful to teach the dog to obey the "down" command in the car. Any animal as large as a Newf can make changing lanes or backing up hazardous by obscuring the driver's rear vision. Also, a dog should not be allowed to ride with his head out the window. This not only interferes with the driver's vision, but can cause injury to the dog's eyes and ears.

Cars parked in the sun become extremely hot, even on mild days. A slightly opened window or windows will not be adequate to cool and ventilate the car sufficiently on warm days. On hot days, a car will become excessively hot even with all the windows open unless it is parked in the shade. If gone for more than a few minutes, one must be aware that a car parked in the shade may be completely in the sun a short while later. It takes only a brief time for a car parked in the sun to become a death trap for a dog.

Frequently, dogs are seen riding in the back of open pickup trucks. There is no way to tether a dog safely in a pickup without running the risk of injury in the event of a sudden stop or a rear end collision. Untethered, the dog faces the same risks and also is free to jump out of the vehicle. Regardless of how well trained a dog might be, a bitch in season or some other attraction can prove to be a fatal lure. If a dog must be carried in a pickup, it should be crated and provided with protection against sun and rain.

Health Care

Newfoundlands have a tendency toward pica (eating non-food items). Many are especially fond of wood, charcoal, or grass. The material actually swallowed seems to be fairly well tolerated by the digestive system. However, some char-

coal briquettes have additives which could prove dangerous, and hardwoods tend to splinter. Grass treated with chemical fertilizers or herbicides is toxic. It is wise to bear in mind these possible hazards if one owns a wood-, charcoal-, or grass-eating Newf.

Stool eating, which may be caused by boredom, a nutritional deficiency, or a lack of sufficient digestive enzymes, can become a habit which continues even after the causative factors have been corrected. Dogs pick up the habit from one another. While the vice has been described as "a rather harmless way a dog recycles food," it is repugnant to humans and could be harmful to a dog consuming waste from dogs with parasites or other diseases spread through contact with feces. Once a dog develops this habit it is important to keep stools picked up and to follow the regimen prescribed by a veterinarian.

Most dogs are attracted to antifreeze which, like any alcohol or petroleum product, is potentially lethal. Families with children are aware of the need for storing automobile, garden, and household products, as well as medicines, out of reach. Childless families adopting a puppy need to follow the same procedure to protect their Newfs.

Poisonous plants, small objects which a dog might swallow or choke on, brittle plastic objects, and chicken and rib bones need to be kept out of reach. Uncooked beef thigh bones are probably safe but cannot be left lying around for prolonged chewing. They become contaminated by bacteria as the marrow and any attached flesh begins to decay.

The need for veterinary attention is often indicated by changes in behavior. Sometimes it takes a day or two for the owner to become aware that a dog is not feeling well. Refusal of a single meal is not going to send one running to the vet, but a second day's refusal or noticeable behavior changes would indicate something is amiss. Projectile diarrhea, bloody diarrhea, persistent vomiting, inability to keep down water, rigidity or paralysis, convulsions, breathing difficulties, unusually heavy panting, bloating, excessive or frothy salivating, and obvious pain are all indications for immediate medical attention.

Dogs are stoics in the face of pain. If a dog is whimpering, crying out, or limping severely he is probably in considerable pain. Reasons for such behavior may not be apparent. It is far better to have the dog examined than to delay seeking advice on what could be a life-threatening problem.

Skin problems make up the largest percentage of client visits for many veterinarians. Because these are not life-threatening problems it is tempting to wait for them to heal by themselves or to try home remedies. If neglected, most skin problems only become worse. It is more economical for the owner and more comfortable for the dog to have skin problems treated before they get out of hand. Skin problems may be caused by fleas and other parasites, both internal and external, and by allergy, fungi, trauma, and irritations. Diagnosis of the causative factor is necessary before appropriate treatment is begun.

The normal body temperature of dogs is 101.5 degrees Farenheit. It is easiest to take a dog's temperature using a rectal thermometer, if someone is available to assist by distracting the dog by petting and talking to him during the process. Begin by lubricating the thermometer with petroleum jelly or tepid water. Then "down" the dog and turn him on his side. While he is being distracted, lift the tail and insert the thermometer. Hold it in place for three to five minutes, then remove it and praise the dog.

Large and giant breeds are more susceptible to orthopedic problems than most smaller breeds. Some of these problems are transmitted genetically, and some seem to be the result of a familial tendency. Some occur as a result of trauma. The usual symptom of an orthopedic problem is lameness. A puppy or dog may limp as the result of a cut pad, a foot fungus, or a minor trauma. If a limp persists beyond a day or two a veterinarian should be consulted. Surgery, rest, or medication may be indicated, depending on the diagnosis, and the sooner started the better.

Limping in the forequarters may be due to osteochondritis dissecans, a condition in which a lesion occurs in the growth area of one of the long bones. It is a juvenile disease. It is thought to be a result of trauma, such as jumping from a raised object, in puppies with a familial tendency toward the disease. If the lesion is severe or if a fragment of bone has chipped off, surgery may be necessary. Less severe cases may be overcome with a restriction of activity.

Another forequarter problem is elbow dysplasia. This is a condition which involves more than one phenomenon. Usually, elbow dysplasia involves failure of certain elbow bones to unite. Surgery is required to remove loose bone.

Long bone disease, or panosteitis, can affect all four limbs. In many cases a limp will "travel" from one leg to any one or all of the others. Like osteochondritis and elbow dysplasia, panosteitis begins in puppyhood. It is considered to be self-limiting and most dogs recover at about one year of age. Analgesics may be prescribed to alleviate discomfort.

Hindquarter lameness is most often associated with hip dysplasia. This is a hereditary disease which ranges in severity from mild cases to extreme ones. A dog with mild or moderate dysplasia may go through life never showing symptoms. Other dogs show symptoms as early as four or five months of age. Common early symptoms include difficulty in getting up from a prone position and "bunny hopping" rather than gaiting. Older dogs with no previous symptoms may show stiffness or have difficulty in getting up after exercise. Hip dysplasia is a progressive disease in which the femoral head becomes misshapen and does not fit tightly into the hip socket. There are surgical procedures to alleviate the discomfort of the disease.

A ruptured cruciate ligament in the stifle (knee) also causes hindquarter lameness. This condition is thought to be caused by trauma. If the rupture is complete the dog usually will put no weight on the leg. With partial ruptures some dogs will show only occasional lameness. Surgery is usually required to repair the injury.

Twenty-five years ago many orthopedic diseases were virtually unknown to the veterinary general practitioner. The increase in popularity of the large and giant breeds since then has brought an increase in knowledge of these diseases and how to diagnose and treat them. Obviously, a veterinarian with a large clientele of giant breeds will have had more experience in radiographing, diagnosing, and treating these diseases. It is worth making an effort to find such a veterinarian, not only because of his or her experience with orthopedics, but because of familiarity with general care and treatment of the giant breeds.

Routine veterinary care includes immunization against the common canine diseases, plus rabies. Initial puppy vaccinations do not provide permanent immunity, and annual booster shots are required for distemper, hepatitis, leptospirosis, tracheobronchitis, and parvovirus. Many localities have laws requiring proof of rabies vaccination.

Parasites

Dogs may host a variety of external and internal parasites. The most common external parasites are fleas, which are seasonal from summer to early winter. Despite the jokes about dogs and fleas, fleas are no joke. They cause great discomfort. Dogs with a heavy infestation or with a flea allergy become frantic with the itching. They scratch and chew on themselves to the point where the skin can become severely damaged.

It is not always possible to find fleas on a heavy-coated dog, but if he is scratching and chewing, they are probably present. Spray, powder, or dip the dog according to the directions on the product you are using. Follow the recommended schedule for repeated treatment through the entire flea season.

If you find a number of pustules or a lesion, it is advisable to have the dog examined by your vet. Without relief from the itching, the dog will irritate these areas to the point where a "hot spot" may develop. The skin exudes a thick, oily substance and becomes very sore and tender. Continued irritation will cause the hot spot to enlarge, and sometimes become infected. Cortisone shots and/or tablets are sometimes prescribed to reduce inflammation and itching. A topical anesthetic or an antibiotic also may be prescribed.

Fleas also spread tapeworm, an internal parasite. The best way to avoid the problems caused by fleas is to keep them under control. Dips, powders, and sprays have been mentioned. Flea baths are effective in killing fleas on a dog but the residual effect is minimal. Flea collars are largely ineffective on Newfs, with their large size and heavy coats.

Ticks are also seasonal. Flea and tick sprays are less effective against ticks than fleas. In areas where ticks are a problem it is advisable to examine the skin frequently to find the ticks before they become engorged.

Mange mites usually infest the skin around the eyes and mouth. The mites cannot be seen, and their presence is indicated by loss of hair. Your vet can prescribe a suitable medication for treatment.

Ear mites are indicated by a foul odor and a rapid buildup of a dark exudate in the ears. The dog may shake his head and scratch his ears. Discovered early, ear mites usually are not difficult to eliminate. An untreated case of long standing may be more difficult to treat successfully.

Roundworm is the most common internal parasite found in dogs. Mature roundworms can be found in most puppies before six weeks of age. Left unchecked, this parasite can severely debilitate a growing pup. Repeated wormings are usually necessary before all adult worms and eggs are expelled.

Hookworm, whipworm, and tapeworm are also intestinal parasites. They are less common than roundworms but are severely debilitating to both puppies and adult dogs. Dogs may become infested with tapeworm by eating fleas that harbor tapeworm eggs. A less common source is uncooked meat. Whipworm and hookworm are contracted from feces of infected dogs or from soil on which such feces have decayed. Whipworm eggs picked up on pads or coat may be licked off and ingested by the dog. Hookworm larva penetrates the dog's pads and enters the bloodstream and ultimately the intestinal tract. Infection can recur easily.

Worming medication for these parasites was once quite hazardous, and of questionable effectiveness. Fortunately there are now safer, more effective treatments. These medications are available only through licensed veterinarians. It is advisable to have your dog's stools checked by your vet every six months and to follow his or her advice for treatment if worms are present. Worming a dog with patent medicines for undiagnosed parasites is taking an unnecessary risk with your dog's health.

Once a dog has contracted hookworm or whipworm, sanitation practices become doubly important. The dog can become reinfected from his own droppings. Your vet can advise you of a regimen to follow to prevent reinfection.

Areas of the country which harbor mosquitoes also harbor heartworm. As the name implies, this is not an intestinal parasite. The infestation is spread by mosquitoes injecting microfilariae, a stage in the life cycle of the heartworm. It may take months before the dog has a buildup of actual worms in the heart. By this time, the process of eradicating the worms becomes a delicate procedure. It is far safer to use preventive measures than to allow the dog to become infected. If you live in an area where there are mosquitoes, see your veterinarian for a medication to be given throughout the mosquito season. The veterinarian may also suggest periodic blood tests to make certain the dog is not infected. It is far safer to treat before the microfilariae mature.

Newfoundland drawings by Alan Riley.

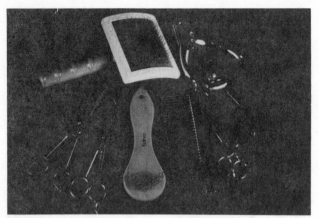

Grooming tools, counterclockwise from the top: slicker, thinning shears, straight edged shears, rake, comb, fine scissors, and two types of nail clippers.

Using thinning shears to trim ear, after edge has been trimmed with straight edged shears. Notice that shears point up. Cutting motion is from down to up.

Puppy with untrimmed ears.

Puppy with ears   trimmed.

Detail of ear.

Detail of ear.

Grooming

Grooming a Newfoundland includes brushing, trimming excess hair from ears and feet, cleaning ears, trimming nails, and scaling teeth. Brushing should be done on a weekly basis, and other grooming chores should be taken care of at the same time.

Brushing prevents the formation of mats in the dog's coat, and removes dead hair which otherwise would be shed on rugs, furniture, and clothing.

Grooming tools include a slicker brush, straight-edged shears with rounded points, thinning shears, small scissors, and nail clippers. A rake, metal dog comb, and tooth scaler are useful as well. (See illustration, page 52.)

It is most comfortable for the groomer if the dog is trained to stand and lie on a sturdy table so the groomer can work standing up. Grooming tables can be purchased but are a rather expensive item for use with only one dog. A heavy picnic table is both large enough and sturdy enough for a Newf. It can be used outdoors in summer and in a garage or basement during colder weather. As an alternative, if your back and knees don't complain, work on the floor. There is a special feeling of closeness which comes from sitting on the floor with your dog and brushing him.

When brushing, work from rear to front and from bottom to top. This is not to say that you brush against the lay of the hair. The hair in front of the slicker brush is lifted by the left hand while the brush goes through the underlayer of hair in the direction in which it grows. After one layer has been brushed, move the left hand forward to release another layer and brush that. To do the back, begin at the base of the tail. To do legs, ribs, and chest, begin at the lowest point and work up. The longer hair on tail, pantaloons, and feathers is done the same way.

Many dogs that otherwise enjoy being brushed do not find it pleasant to have the pantaloons done. Be especially careful in the area of the genitals so your dog will not have reason to resist having the pantaloons worked on. The wire teeth of a slicker brush can cause injury or great discomfort in this delicate area. It is best to cover the testicles or vulva area with one hand while brushing near it.

Ears and feet are trimmed for neatness. How often this will need to be done depends upon the owner's tastes, and how fast the hair grows on the individual dog. Begin on the

ears by cutting along the edge of the ear flap with the straight-edged shears. Then use thinning shears to shorten the hair on the flap itself. This is done by moving the thinning shears from the tip of the ear toward the skull while snipping rapidly. Only a small amount of hair will be removed with each snip. This process needs to be repeated a number of times in order to trim the whole ear. It takes a bit of practice, but after a few haircuts, you can become quite proficient.

Feet are trimmed by using the straight-edged shears to

Jill Stackhouse uses a slicker on Steamboat's Chocolate Sundae, bred and owned by Betty Stackhouse. Jill's left hand pushes the hair up at the starting point of the downward stroke.

Loose mats may be pulled apart.

Finished foot (right) has been trimmed on top, along edges, and between pads. It is best to trim nails after excess hair has been removed.

trace the outline of the foot and to trim the hair between the pads. Left to grow, this hair will cover the pads and reduce the dog's traction on slippery surfaces. Long hair also collects mud and dust. Snow clings to it and forms snowballs. The long hair on the upper foot is also trimmed. Brush or comb it straight up, then use the thinning shears to shorten it.

Some coats tend to mat in the neck area under the jaw. Matting can be reduced by trimming this area. Use the straight-edged shears by cutting upward. Some mats can be removed simply by pulling them apart. Begin with the outer hair on one side of the mat and pull a few hairs at a time. Brush with the slicker brush after the hairs have been separated.

Larger, thicker mats sometimes can be pulled apart if the outside edge is first cut straight across. Then proceed as above.

The most difficult mats to remove are those which cover a wide area and/or those which extend down to the skin. Special care should be taken when cutting this kind of mat. It can seem as if you are cutting hair when you are actually cutting the skin. Always work in a very good light, use the small scissors, and proceed slowly. Cut only a few hairs at a time, as far from the skin as possible. This will release a small section of the mat. Lift this section so you can see what you are cutting and snip a few more hairs. Sometimes it becomes difficult to see what you will be cutting. In this case, approach the mat from another side. Occasionally you will need to cut from all sides of a mat before the central hairs will be free enough so that you can finally remove the entire mat.

As with most problems, prevention is preferable to a cure. A thorough weekly brushing will all but eliminate a buildup of mats. Brushing also keeps the coat clean.

Unless a Newf is being shown, it is not necessary to give baths regularly. One or two baths a year are sufficient for a Newf that is kept well groomed through weekly brushing.

Healthy coats have a pleasant odor. A few Newfs manage to keep the hair under the "chin" damp and they begin to smell like a sour towel. This can be avoided by keeping the hair in that area short. If your dog has an unpleasant odor and the hair on his back appears oily, it may be due to seborrhea. A bath will not eliminate the problem. The condition should be treated by a vet.

When a bath is needed, do a thorough grooming first. Remove mats and trim feet and ears. Brush out all loose hair. It may seem as if it would be more pleasant to groom after the dog is clean, but, unfortunately, bathing causes loose hair to mat and makes mats already in the coat harder to remove. Another brushing is the final step after a bath. This will remove small mats which may have gone unnoticed or which formed in dead hair not removed before the bath. It also gives the dog a "finished" appearance.

There is a bewildering array of coat care products avail-

able for dogs. For general care, shampoo is the only necessity. While any mild shampoo will clean the coat, dog shampoos are worth the extra cost. Dog hair has a different acidity/alkalinity level from that of human hair, and canine shampoos are formulated to compensate for this difference. You may wish to choose a product designed specifically for black dogs, which does not contain dyes or coloring agents but highlights the black coat.

It is easiest to bathe a Newf outdoors. If possible, connect a hose to a sink or laundry tub with warm water available. Cold water can be used but is far less effective in penetrating a Newf's oily coat. Find a location where your hose will reach and where the dog can be tied up. Prepare everything before securing the dog. Attach a trigger spray nozzle to the hose and adjust the water temperature. Most dog shampoos come in squeeze bottles, so if tipped over they will not spill. Have the shampoo ready. Finally, attach the dog to his lead and tether him.

Wet the dog as thoroughly as possible with warm water, then apply shampoo. You will find that as the shampoo is applied, it will be possible to wet areas which repelled water during the initial spraying. Spray the dog with the hose again and apply more shampoo. When the dog is thoroughly wet and covered with shampoo, rub in the lather.

When using the spray near the ear, grasp the ear at its base and hold it shut, so that water will not go inside. The face should not be shampooed nor sprayed, but should be cleaned with a damp cloth.

Rinse carefully and thoroughly. Soap residue can cause itching and irritation. Release the dog to shake. In warm weather he can be left to dry outdoors. In cooler weather he should be brought inside. Newfs can be bathed outdoors in weather as cool as forty degrees but should not be left out longer than necessary to shake off excess water. This breed will swim in icy water with no ill effects, because the natural oil in the coat prevents the water from coming in contact with the skin. Bathing temporarily removes the oil. A coat wet to the skin will cause the dog to become chilled. In weather below forty degrees bathing should be done indoors.

Dog grooming parlors and some veterinary clinics and boarding kennels have bathing facilities. Their fees are an alternative to using the family bathtub, with the ensuing mess to clean up.

Nail trimming, like all grooming procedures, should begin in puppyhood. Long nails cause discomfort and result in lack of traction on slippery surfaces. Also, they can distort the feet. Dogs do not like having their feet handled and are especially wary when their nails are involved. A small puppy usually is manageable on your lap, but if he will not submit to having his nails worked on, get someone to distract him while you concentrate on trimming the nails. It is also helpful to handle a puppy's feet when petting him so that he gets used to being touched in that area.

An objecting dog the size of an adult Newf can make the task of nail trimming almost impossible for the owner. If you have had no experience in trimming nails, it would be advisable to have a professional groomer or veterinarian cut them the first time. Watch the process and ask questions so you can do it yourself the next time. If a tranquilizer was necessary, you may want to tranquilize the dog the first time or two on your own. This will give you and the dog a chance to get used to the process without establishing a routine of dog vs. owner.

When trimming nails, the main concern is to avoid cutting the quick, which is a very sensitive area. Cutting it not only causes the dog pain, but also causes the nail to bleed. A styptic pencil or ferrous sulphate powder should be kept with your nail trimmer so it will be available if needed.

If your Newf has white feet, his nails may be translucent. The quick will appear as a pinkish "tube" inside the nail, and it will not be difficult to tell how far the nail may be cut safely without touching the quick. Unfortunately, the quick cannot be seen through the black outer layer on the nails of most Newfs. For this reason, the nails should be cut back by taking off thin slices. The inside of the nail is grayish-white in color. The quick appears as a blackish spot in the center. When paring off thin layers, you will see this spot appear before you cut into it. As soon as you see it, stop trimming. If the dog's nails are still too long, wait a week and trim them again. The quick will have receded slightly during this time.

Obviously, it is best not to let the nails become overgrown, but if it happens, be patient. It is better to take off a little of the excess once a week than to cut into the quick. Even the most cooperative dog will become reluctant to have his nails worked on once this happens.

Ears should be kept clean. Commercial products for ear cleaning are available but it is more economical to use cotton balls dipped in isopropyl alcohol. After dipping, be sure to squeeze out most of the moisture so it will not drip into the ear. Then swab, getting into the nooks and crannies without penetrating too deeply into the ear canal. A weekly check will show whether there is an accumulation of waxy substance. If there is a "cheesy" odor or rapid buildup of exudate, have the ears checked by the vet.

Tooth scaling prevents a buildup of tartar and helps keep teeth and gums healthy. It is advisable to have the process demonstrated before attempting it. Your vet or a dog groomer can show you how it is done.

While the Newfoundland is not an "easy care" breed when it comes to grooming, it is not one which needs daily maintenance. Weekly grooming is the ideal rather than a rigid necessity. A Newf will not become a hopeless mess if he misses a few grooming sessions.

If approached with the dog's comfort in mind, so that he learns to enjoy it, grooming becomes a bonding experience between dog and owner. It is one that many Newf owners would not trade for an "easy care" dog.

A jacket made from brushed out Newfoundland undercoat. The color of the dead hair ranges from gray to brown. The jacket is very warm and lightweight.

Ch. Newfport's Outward Bound, bred and owned by Mae and Jack Bernhard. "Byron," shown here on his grooming table at the 1982 NCA National Specialty, has been groomed to perfection.

Ch. Shadybrook's Mama Bear, C.D., W.R.D., bred and owned by Jeri and Richard Krokum, leaps from a dock to retrieve a bumper at an NCA Water Test.

Until he was ten years old, Seamount Gunny Sgt. Sam gave exhilarating rides to his owner's children and their friends as he ran beside Alex Polson (on bicycle). In a hilly neighborhood, Sam developed his own braking system by pressing against the shafts on the downhill run. Courtesy Sunset Magazine.

The Newfoundland in Competition

The Working Newfoundland

Purebred dogs of today exhibit characteristics, developed through selective breeding, which enable them to fulfill specific roles in human society. Certain temperamental and physical characteristics are required of a breed in order that it may do its required task, whether it be guarding, herding, retrieving, varmint hunting, or finding game.

The Newfoundland is classified by the AKC as a member of the Working Group. His tasks in the past have included pulling carts and sleds, carrying backpacks, and helping the fishermen of Newfoundland pull in their heavy nets. These were jobs requiring strength, endurance, and patience—the same traits evident in our present-day Newfs.

Newfoundland owners today enjoy seeing the working abilities of their dogs in recreational and competitive activities. The Newfoundland Club of America established a Working Dog Committee in order to help maintain and promote the working abilities of the breed. The committee, over a period of many years, has developed and revised manuals which provide assistance in training Newfs for water and draft work. The committee also developed a series of exercises and rules for Water Tests and carting competitions. Work is currently in progress on a backpacking manual and rules for earning a backpacking certificate.

The first Newfoundland Club of America Water Test was held in Horton, Michigan, in July 1973. Water competitions had been held in the United States as early as 1929, but the 1973 test was the first at which Water Dog and Water Rescue Dog title certificates were awarded by the Newfoundland Club of America. Three dogs passed the Junior Division exercises and one also passed the Senior Division exercises the same day.

Since that day, Water Tests have been held in at least nine states. Several tests are held each year in different regions, making it possible for Newfs to earn the titles of Water Dog (W.D.) and Water Rescue Dog (W.R.D.). A Water Test is sometimes included in the annual Newfoundland Club of America National Specialty Show weekend.

The title "Water Dog" is awarded to Newfs passing the following exercises in the Junior Division:

1. Basic Control Off-Lead: Heeling off lead, performing a recall and doing the long down exercises demonstrate that the dog has been trained in basic control.

2. Single Retrieve: The dog retrieves, and returns to the handler, a boat bumper thrown at least thirty feet from shore.

3. Drop Retrieve: The dog is sent to retrieve a life jacket or boat cushion dropped by a steward on the seaward side of a boat at least fifty feet from the shore.

4. Take a Line: The dog is sent with a line in his mouth to a steward standing out approximately fifty feet from the shore.

5. Tow a Boat: The dog tows a boat, using the painter to which a bumper has been attached, along the shore for a distance of fifty feet. He is accompanied by his handler.

6. Swim with Handler: Dog and handler swim out twenty feet beyond wading depth and return to shore with the dog towing the handler to shore.

Senior Division Exercises leading to the "Water Rescue Dog" title are:

1. Retrieve Off a Boat: The dog dives from a boat to retrieve a canoe paddle thrown about ten feet from the boat.

2. Take a Line/Tow a Boat: The dog is sent with a line in his mouth to a steward in a boat about seventy-five feet from shore. The dog is to tow the boat to shore after the steward has taken the line from him.

3. Take a Lifering: The dog is sent to take a lifering to one of three stewards approximately seventy-five feet from shore and spaced thirty feet apart. The Water Test judge designates to which steward the ring should be taken.

4. Directed Retrieve: The dog is sent to retrieve two objects, one at a time and in the sequence directed by the Water Test judge, which have been dropped by a steward from a boat. The objects are dropped fifty feet from shore and fifty feet apart.

5. Rescue: The dog is to dive from a boat fifty feet from shore from which his handler has "fallen," swim to the handler and tow him/her back to boat or shore.

6. Underwater Retrieve: The dog retrieves, either by ducking under water or by pawing to shore, an object submerged at his belly depth.

Achieving the water titles is the result of many hours of training and practice. The exercises are based upon the Newf's natural instincts, but standards of performance are rigorous and must be met to the point of completion of each exercise in order for the dog to pass. A complete booklet of the regulations and exercises for the Water Tests can be obtained from the N.C.A.

The dog cart, once a symbol of canine labor, is now a symbol of pleasure for Newfs and their young passengers. Most Newfs love to pull and, once used to the rattling and bumping of a cart behind them, look forward eagerly to getting hitched up. Some Newfs take to the cart the first time they are put in the traces.

Above, Ch. Lucabuc's Thursday's Child, C.D.X., W.R.D., owned by Kathy Mitchell, tows a boat to land after delivering the line, in the Senior Division "Tow-a-Boat" exercise.

Above, NCA Water Test. Here, Ch. Shadybrook's Lil Pebbles, C.D.X., W.D., triumphantly brings in a boat cushion for the Junior Division "Drop Retrieve" exercise.

Above, Sweetbay's Dylan, W.R.D., bred and owned by Judy and Ellis Adler, tows a steward to shore after carrying a lifering to her in the Senior Division "Lifering" exercise.

Above, Gaby Kennedy points to a submerged object for Salty Dog's Peter Duncan, C.D., W.R.D., in the Senior Division "Underwater Retrieve." Duncan was bred by his owner.

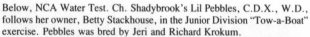

Below, NCA Water Test. Ch. Shadybrook's Lil Pebbles, C.D.X., W.D., follows her owner, Betty Stackhouse, in the Junior Division "Tow-a-Boat" exercise. Pebbles was bred by Jeri and Richard Krokum.

Below, Ch. Halirock's Seamount Hannah and Seamount Whaleboat Teddy cross a mountain stream while backpacking with their owner, Alan Riley.

The Newfoundland Club of America offers a carting competition each year at its National Specialty Show. Carts and handlers, often decorated and costumed, go through a series of exercises to demonstrate the dogs' abilities to respond to commands and to maneuver successfully. Exercises include starting, stopping, right and left turns, and backing up. An interesting variety of carts, some of which have been transported across the country for the event, and the opportunity to watch the Newfs perform a traditional task, make the carting competition a popular spectator attraction at the Specialty Show.

Proper balance, light weight, and wheels which move easily are important factors in a suitable dog cart. A comfortable harness and hitching arrangement are also important. The Draft Equipment Guide available from the Newfoundland Club of America includes charts, patterns, and guides for making equipment, mail order sources for ready-made equipment, and guidelines for working with draft dogs.

With an increased number of people enjoying wilderness camping and hiking, Newf owners are learning the pleasure and value of their pets as trail companions. In wild lands it is essential that dogs be trained in trail, camp, and wilderness manners so they will not be a nuisance or a hazard to wildlife, the environment, other hikers, or their owner.

One great pleasure of hiking with a trained dog is the peer relationship which can be achieved between dog and owner. A sensitive owner will find that close attention to the dog's behavior increases his or her awareness, through the acute senses of the dog, of what is occurring in a strange environment.

Newfoundlands are natural retrievers and can be used for duck hunting. Most are "soft mouthed" and will not damage birds brought to shore.

Several years ago a woman bought a Newf with only grudging acquiescence from her husband, who wanted a sporting breed for duck hunting. The man totally ignored the dog for two years. One fall day, on impulse, he took the dog hunting with him. The Newf watched as the first duck was felled, noting where it had dropped. He was ordered to retrieve it. Despite the fact that he had never been trained, the dog plunged into the water, but returned to shore without the bird. The owner, in disgust, watched the Newf leave the water and retreat to a high bank above the shore. Then, to his amazement, he saw the dog dive from the bank into the water, swim directly to the duck, and return it to shore. From that day on, the Newf had two devoted owners.

Obedience Training

Young Newfoundlands exhibit the same exuberance as the youngsters of less placid breeds, but the size and weight of a Newfie pup makes early training more important than for a smaller breed. Most obedience groups accept puppies into their classes at six months of age. Some hold "Kindergarten Puppy Training" (KPT) classes for younger puppies, which are a kind of canine preschool. It is an advantage to both puppy and owner to attend such a session if a puppy's age qualifies him at the time classes begin. If you cannot take your dog to a puppy class, enroll him in a regular obedience class as soon as possible after he reaches the minimum age.

Basic obedience teaches you to teach the dog to: heel, sit, stay, lie down, stand still, and come. Some individuals have a natural ability to train dogs and can teach their dogs the basic commands without help. There is still an advantage in attending a class, however. The dogs learn to behave amid the distractions of other dogs and people, and to obey even when away from familiar surroundings. The training methods have been honed to a high degree of efficiency and serve for further training, once dog and owner have completed the series of classes.

If you plan to attend an obedience class, check the credentials of the trainer or trainers. Most large urban areas have obedience training clubs (with non-profit status) that offer classes. The clubs' trainers are qualified by experience in training their own dogs and through apprenticeship programs with other trainers.

There are also excellent trainers who hold private classes. When checking the trainer's credentials, ask how many dogs he or she has trained to AKC obedience titles. The answer should be more than one or two. Also ask for the names of dog owners who have participated in the trainer's classes. You may wish to inquire as to their satisfaction with the training sessions.

Newfoundlands have a desire to please and are pleasant dogs to work with in obedience. It is easy to get caught up in obedience training as a sport. If you find the work satisfying and enjoy the social activity of working and training with others, you may want to work toward AKC titles.

Obedience Trials are held at most all-breed shows, with three levels of competition: *Novice, Open,* and *Utility. Novice* is for dogs that have completed the basic training provided in beginning obedience and are working toward the Companion Dog (C.D.) title. The six exercises in Novice work are: heel on leash, stand for examination, heel free (off leash), recall (come on command), long sit (one minute), and long down (three minutes). *Open* competition is for dogs that have completed the second stage of training. The work includes the following exercises: heel free, drop on recall, retrieve on flat (retrieve a dumbbell), retrieve over the high jump, broad jump, long sit (three minutes), and long down (five minutes). These dogs are working toward the Companion Dog Excellent (C.D.X.) title. *Utility* is the highest title offered, and the work includes: signal exercise, scent discrimination, directed retrieve, directed jumping, and group examination (group stand). Dogs in this class are working toward the Utility Dog (U.D.) title.

Ch. Kilyka's Colossus, U.D., W.R.D., retrieves a dumbbell over a jump.

Ch. Dryad's Lord Nelson, U.D.T., bred by Lily Fulton and owned by Betty McDonnell. Nelson sired two National Specialty Best-of-Breed winners as well as numerous champion and obedience-titled Newfs.

Ch. Kilyka's Calypso, U.D.T.X., W.R.D., D.D., bred and owned by Betty McDonnell, shown tracking with her owner. Calypso is the only Newfoundland to hold all of these titles, as well as "Versatility Newf."

Gaby Kennedy holds the object Duncan has retrieved and presented to her, as the dog shakes.

At each level of obedience work, dogs must earn 170 out of 200 points in three separate trials in order to be awarded a title for that level. Dogs that have earned the Utility Dog title may continue to compete in Open and Utility Classes for class prizes. Handlers with highly competitive scores may set their sights on earning points toward the highly esteemed Obedience Trial Champion title.

Tracking Dog (T.D.) titles may also be earned. In tracking exercises, the dog is expected to demonstrate his ability to follow human scent on a course where weather, lay of the land, ground cover, and wind must be taken into consideration.

Obedience can be enjoyed as a competitive sport in which a handler and his dog vie with others for high scores and for one of four placement ribbons awarded in each class, or a handler may choose to compete for the sense of achievement gained from earning passing scores, and eventually earn a title or titles for his or her Newf.

Show Competition

Showing dogs has become increasingly popular as a sport. But dog shows have a serious aspect as well. The show ring holds the future of each breed. It is an arena in which breeders and exhibitors demonstrate and test the success of breeding programs. Dogs that become known for consistent wins are often in demand as stud dogs. Puppies from top winning bitches are sought after. These are the animals whose genes become widely disseminated and affect future generations. Judges hold an awesome responsibility in making their selections.

Dog show judges are approved by The American Kennel Club to judge specific breeds. When judging, they try to determine which dog and bitch, according to the breed Standard, are the best representatives of their breed. To do this, a judge examines each entry by looking at the overall outline of the dog and by feeling the dog's structure. Each entry is gaited to show its movement from the front, rear, and side.

Shows offer six classes for dogs and six classes for bitches in each breed. The winner of each class competes against the winners of the same sex from the other classes for Winners Dog or Winners Bitch awards. Winners Dog and Winners Bitch compete with any champions in their breed, for Best of Breed and Best of Opposite Sex. They also compete against each other for Best of Winners. The Newfoundland awarded Best of Breed then competes with other Working Group breed winners for Working Group placement, and the winner of the Working Group goes on to compete against winners of the six other Groups for the Best in Show award.

Winners Dog and Winners Bitch receive points toward championship titles. The number of points won at a given show depends upon the number of dogs competing and the region of the country in which they are being shown. Seven regional divisions each have a schedule showing how many dogs must compete in order to win a certain number of points. The number of points which may be earned at a single show ranges from one to five. The point schedule is revised annually by the AKC. To earn a championship, a dog must win a total of fifteen points, with major wins under at least two different judges. Three to five points are awarded for a major win.

The AKC maintains cumulative records of the points a dog has won and automatically awards a Championship Certificate when the requirements have been met. Exhibitors should keep all ribbons and awards from shows at which their dogs have placed, and also should keep a record of the points their dogs have won.

It is thought that the first championship title awarded to a Newfoundland in the United States was won by a dog named Sam in 1883. The aegis and significance of this title are unknown, as AKC records show that the first Championship Certificate was awarded to Major II in 1913.

It was not until the late 1960s and early 1970s that Newfs could be found at most large dog shows. Even today, entries do not compare with those of more popular breeds, yet quite a number of Newfs finish their championships each year. In 1983, for example, the AKC recorded 128 new Newfoundland champions.

If you are interested in showing your Newfoundland, whether a puppy or an adult, it is a good idea to have your dog evaluated for his show potential before investing the time and funds required to show him properly. Begin with your dog's breeder, if he or she lives nearby. Ask other Newf fanciers for their opinions. Professional handlers or experts in other breeds may not be familiar with Newfoundlands but they can tell you if your dog is well put together and moves properly.

If you have been encouraged to show your Newf, you will need to begin learning about shows and showing. Study the breed Standard so you will be able to identify the strengths and weaknesses of your dog. Write to the AKC for a copy of "Rules Applying to Registration and Dog Shows." Every dog show exhibitor is responsible for knowing these rules. Attend dog shows and watch the Newfoundlands and other breeds being judged.

You will need to learn how to train your dog to gait and stand to be examined. You will need to know how to handle your dog and present him to his best advantage. Grooming for shows requires new learning, and developing a finesse not required for pet grooming.

If there is a regional Newfoundland club in your area, there will be individuals willing to help you in preparing to show your Newf. Some clubs hold handling classes and grooming sessions for new members. Most regional clubs hold annual fun matches. These serve as practice shows for dogs and handlers.

Shipway's Avalon Holly, American and Canadian U.D.T., W.R.D., bred by Ann Sher and owned by Claire Carr, became the first Newf to earn the NCA Water Dog (W.D.) and Water Rescue Dog (W.R.D.) titles. Holly passed both Junior and Senior Divisions at the first Water Test at which titles were awarded (1973).

All-breed fun matches also offer an opportunity to practice showing your Newf. Information on upcoming matches may be found in newspaper want ads or in pet columns. Veterinary and pet shop bulletin boards are also sources of information on fun matches.

The best preparation for showing is to attend a handling class. These are offered by breed clubs or by professional handlers. You will be trained in gaiting and stacking (posing) your dog, and will learn ring procedure, show protocol, and how to enter shows.

Handling classes are often listed in the pet column section of newspaper want ads. If you cannot find such a listing, try calling boarding and breeding kennels listed in the classified section of the telephone directory. Some of these kennel owners are show exhibitors and may know of clubs or individuals offering classes.

The dog fancy is like a communications network. Anyone seeking information or help can find it if he or she is persistent. A call to one individual may not offer the information you need, but chances are excellent that a second or third call will offer referrals to others who can help.

Seasoned exhibitors often wait until a dog is somewhat mature before showing him. With most Newfs, this means waiting until the dog is two years or older. If you are eager to start showing while your dog is a puppy or a yearling, do not be disappointed if he does not make any big wins. Unless a puppy or youngster is truly outstanding or unusually well developed for his age, he will not be ready to compete against older, more mature dogs for the points. Consider the first year of showing as experience for you and your dog. If you win occasionally, you will be fortunate. As long as showing is fun for you, win or lose, and you are convinced that your dog is worthy of being shown, the early ring experience will serve you and your dog well when the time comes for him to take his place in the winners lineup.

Mike and Sandee Lovett's Newfs, hitched and waiting for wood to be split and loaded.

American and Canadian Ch. Seamount Jonah of Pouch Cove, bred by David and Peggy Helming, with his owner Jo Ann Riley at an all-breed handling class. These classes offer training and ring experience for dogs and owners. Jonah is a Group-placing dog.

63

Four-week-old Newfoundland puppy from Little Bear Kennels.

Breeding and Whelping

The only valid reason for breeding is to perpetuate and enhance the best qualities of the breed. The purpose of breeding is not to produce pets to sell. To be a breeder requires experience, study, and a broad knowledge of the breed. A breeder should be knowledgeable about genetic defects and their transmission, and should be familiar with pedigrees and bloodlines. He or she should be able to recognize the faults in his or her own bitch to determine whether she is of breeding quality, and should know how and where to find a stud to compensate for any faults the bitch may have.

Raising a litter of puppies requires a great deal of time. Undertaking a breeding requires a significant cash outlay even before the puppies are whelped. Veterinary fees for prenatal care, stud fees, costs for shipping or transporting the bitch to the stud, long distance telephone charges, costs of constructing a whelping box and acquiring the necessary equipment (bedding, heat lamp, heating pad, and scales) are only the beginning. Whelping and post-partum veterinary costs are routinely incurred, even if no problems develop with the dam or the litter. The fee for a Caesarian section, if needed, and veterinary care for sick puppies or a sick dam make these costs skyrocket. Additional pens, food and feeding equipment, litter registration fees, worming, and puppy immunizations are all necessary expenses in raising a litter.

Assuming all goes well with a normal sized litter, the breeder may cover expenses when the puppies are sold. But even then, the costs may not be over. Today's puppy buyers are aware of hip dysplasia and other congenital problems. Most buyers expect a guarantee of refund or replacement if their puppy is disabled by such a defect. Funds should be set aside for the duration of the guarantee period to cover refunds, should they become necessary.

It is often difficult for a beginning breeder to sell puppies. Unsold pups held for several weeks or months require a considerable outlay in feeding, additional immunizations, and advertising costs. If a breeder is successful in selling a small litter of only two or three pups, the costs of breeding and raising them probably will not be covered.

Showing, membership in a regional Newfoundland club and/or an all breed club, and association with other Newf fanciers can help provide knowledge and experience with Newfoundlands which will be of help to the prospective breeder. Fellow fanciers often are eager to assist new breeders who are determined to perpetuate the best of the breed.

The breeding life of a bitch begins when she comes into season for the first time at the age of ten to sixteen months. Thereafter, she will come in season at roughly six month intervals. Fertility increases from puberty to full maturity and then declines until a state of total sterility is reached in old age.

The length of the season varies from eighteen to twenty-one days. The first indication is a pronounced swelling of the vulva with coincidental bleeding (called "showing color") for about the first seven to nine days. The discharge gradually turns to a creamy color, and it is during this phase (estrus), from about the tenth to fifteenth days, that the bitch is ovulating and is receptive to the male. Since many Newf bitches continue to show color through the receptive period, color alone should not be used to determine when a bitch is ready to be bred. The ripe, unfertilized ova survive for about seventy-two hours. If fertilization doesn't occur, the ova die and are discharged. If fertilization does take place, each ovum attaches itself to the walls of the uterus, a membrane forms to seal it off, and a fetus develops from it.

Following the estrus phase, the bitch is still in season until about the twenty-first day and will continue to be attractive to males, although she will usually fight them off as she did the first few days. Nevertheless, to avoid accidental mating, the bitch must be confined for the entire period. Virtual imprisonment is necessary, for male dogs display uncanny abilities in their efforts to reach a bitch in season.

Unless a bitch is physically mature—well beyond the puppy stage when she has her first season—breeding should be delayed until at least her second season. Furthermore, even though it is possible for a bitch to conceive twice a year, for her own health she should not be bred more than once a year.

Two or three months before a bitch is to be mated, her physical condition should be considered carefully. If she is too thin, provide a rich, balanced diet plus the regular exercise needed to develop strong, supple muscles. Daily exercise is as necessary for the too-thin bitch as for the too-fat one, although the latter will need more exercise and at a brisker pace, as well as a reduction of food, if she is to be brought to optimum condition. A prospective brood bitch should be given booster shots with a combination vaccine for distemper, hepatitis, leptospirosis, parvovirus, and tracheobronchitis. She also should be vaccinated for rabies. A month before her season is due, a veterinarian should examine a stool specimen for worms. If there is evidence of infestation, the bitch should be wormed.

A dog may be used at stud from the time he reaches physical maturity well into old age. For the safety of the stud dog, it is wise to have at least one experienced person assist with breedings. Bitches should be securely held, perhaps muzzled. This is to prevent injury from a bitch biting out of fear or pain. Furthermore, a bitch may need to be supported to prevent injury to the stud from any attempt to sit or get away during a breeding. Without this support a bitch might be overpowered by a stud dog's weight. She might also attempt to escape because of pain or excitement.

If a stud dog owner accepts a bitch for breeding, he must make every attempt to get natural breedings. As a last resort artificial insemination can be accomplished by a veterinarian. If a bitch is ovulating, artificial insemination can be just as successful as a natural breeding.

It is general practice to breed a bitch twice, skipping a day between breedings. If the bitch is still receptive, a third breeding may be attempted in another forty-eight hours. Usually the first service will be successful. However, if it is not, in most cases an additional service is given free, provided the stud dog is still in the possession of the same owner. If the bitch misses, it may be because her cycle varies widely from normal. Through microscopic examination, a veterinarian can determine when the bitch is entering the estrus phase and thus is likely to conceive.

The owner of the stud should provide a stud service contract. Stud fees and the date they are payable should be negotiated in advance. The litter registration application is completed only after the puppies are whelped, and it must be signed by the owner of the stud as well as the owner of the bitch. Registration forms may be secured by writing The American Kennel Club.

In a normal pregnancy there is visible enlargement of the abdomen by the end of the fifth week. By palpation (feeling with the fingers) a veterinarian may be able to distinguish developing puppies as early as three weeks after mating, but it is unwise for a novice to poke and prod to try to detect the presence of unborn puppies.

The gestation period normally lasts nine weeks, although it may vary from sixty-one to sixty-five days. If it goes beyond sixty-five days from the date of mating, a veterinarian should be consulted.

During the first four or five weeks, the bitch should be permitted her normal amount of activity. As she becomes heavier, she should be walked on leash, but strenuous running and jumping should be avoided. Her diet should be increased after it is known that she is in whelp, and it can be divided into several small meals as she approaches her whelping date.

A whelping box should be secured about two weeks before the puppies are due, and the bitch should be introduced to it so that she will be accustomed to it by the time the puppies arrive. The box should be approximately four feet by six feet with a side wall construction which will confine small puppies and provide a sheltered nook to prevent crushing or smothering by the dam. (See Illustration.)

Forty-eight to seventy-two hours before the litter is to be whelped, a definite change in the shape of the abdomen may be noted. As the time becomes imminent, the bitch probably will scratch and root at her bedding in an effort to make a nest, and may refuse food and ask to be let out every few minutes. But the surest sign is a drop in temperature to ninety-nine degrees about twelve hours before labor begins. The bitch will sit and pant. When hard labor actually begins, the bitch's abdomen and flanks will contract sharply as she attempts to expel a puppy, then rest for a while and try again. Someone should stay with the bitch the entire time that whelping is taking place, and if she appears to be having unusual difficulties, a veterinarian should be called.

Puppies usually are born head first, though some may be born feet first with no difficulty encountered. Each puppy is enclosed in a separate membranous sac that the bitch will remove with her teeth. She will sever the umbilical cord which will be attached to the soft, spongy afterbirth that is expelled right after the puppy emerges. Usually the bitch will attempt to eat the afterbirth. It is necessary to watch and make sure an afterbirth is expelled for each puppy whelped. If afterbirth is retained, the bitch may develop peritonitis and die.

It is imperative to get the new whelp breathing. You will know it is breathing when it lets out a cry. If the bitch is not attempting to clean her puppy—and often maternal instincts are delayed with first litters—take the newborn and give it a brisk rubdown with a heavy towel, holding the puppy's head down so that any fluids can drain from the throat. Time is critical, and breathing must not be delayed. If initial efforts fail, take the skin on the nape of the neck and, rotating your wrist, twist left and right and repeat until you get a cry of life. Another way to stimulate breathing is to put a few drops of brandy on the whelp's tongue. A last resort effort is to blow gently in the pup's mouth to inflate his lungs. Many a "stillborn" has been revived by persistence.

The newborn immediately should be eager to nurse. It is important that each pup get some of the bitch's colostrum, or first milk, for it will provide necessary early immunity. You can assist any pups that are not nursing by squeezing some milk to the surface and then opening the pup's mouth for the entrance of the teat. Hold the pup until he is actively sucking.

When the bitch is ready to expel another whelp, those already born can be placed in a box lined with clean towels and warmed by a heat lamp from above. Puppies are unable to regulate their own temperatures for the first week or so, and they must not be allowed to chill.

While the bitch is not in labor or having contractions, she should be offered cool, fresh water. If the whelping continues over a period of several hours, she may be offered small amounts of food to help keep up her strength.

Whelping sometimes continues for as long as twenty-four hours for a very large litter, but a litter of two or three puppies may be whelped in a few hours. When the bitch settles down, and is content to sleep with her litter, it usually indicates that all have been whelped. (The number of puppies in an average Newfoundland litter is eight.) Within twelve hours after whelping, the bitch should be taken to the vet, who will determine if she has retained any puppies. The vet will probably give her a shot of oxytocin to help her uterus to contract and expel any retained afterbirths.

Whelping Timetable
Hannah ex Andrew
8/19/76

This is a whelping chart for the bitch. It is completed in addition to the chart for the puppies. Unusual behavior such as whining, prolonged straining, or the appearance of fresh blood should be noted.

Also, the time that contractions or other events occur should be noted. Such information is important in determining when to call the veterinarian and will help him to know if assistance is needed.

Time	Comment
10:25 pm	Contractions; fluid; puppy whelped
12:55 am	Contraction; puppy whelped
2:10	Contractions (2)
2:15	Contraction
2:20	Contraction; puppy whelped
4:50	Contraction
4:55	Puppy whelped
6:50	Possible contraction

Time	Comment
7:30	Pitocin administered per veterinarian's advice
8:02	Contractions
8:32	3 or 4 good contractions
8:42	Contractions
9:05	Small contraction
9:30	Took Hannah to vet. X-ray showed no more pups.
10:00 am	Final dose of pitocin administered by vet.

Whelping Record
Hannah ex Jupiter
7/17/74

This is a typical whelping record, to be charted as the litter is whelped. Unexpelled placentas may require antibiotic treatment. Yarn tied on immediately after each pup is whelped makes it possible to identify pups—in this case, the pup that died three days later as the one that had to be revived with suction and hot (not scalding) water.

Time Whelped	Sex	ID Marking	Placenta Expelled	Weight	Comments
2:00 pm	M	Red	No	1½ lbs.	Found teat— nursed strongly
2:25	F	Pink	No	1¼	
4:15	M	Green	No	1¼	Black fluid; whelped without sac
6:30	M	Blue	Yes	1¼	
6:40	F	Yellow	?	1¼	
7:25	F	White	No	1¼	
9:05	F	Turquoise	Yes	1	
10:55	M	Lavender	Yes	1⅛	Filled with fluid. Sucked and put in hot water—began breathing.
11:20	M	Orange	Yes	1¼	
1:05 am	M	Purple	Yes	1½	
3:00	F		Yes		Filled with fluid; unable to start breathing.

Weight Chart
Hannah ex Jupiter

This chart shows a typical growth pattern for Newfoundland puppies. Puppies should be weighed daily for the first two or three weeks, then semi-weekly until eight weeks. There is no significant relationship between birth weight and adult size. Even by the time the puppies are eight weeks of age, predicting ultimate size is simply guesswork. Many large puppies mature to be average size adults, while a small puppy may turn out to be above average.

Newfoundland puppies are often so similar at birth that breeders reguarly identify them by tying different colors of yarn around their necks. Care must be taken to tie a square knot that will not tighten, and also to change yarn periodically as the pups' necks become larger. The colors assigned the pups below were selected at birth.

Puppy Identification Markings						*Age in Weeks*				
	Birth	1	2	3	4	5	6	7	8
Red (M)	1½ lbs	2	3	6	9	11	15	18½	22
Pink (F)	1¼	2½	4	6	9	11	14	17½	21
Green (M)	1¼	2	4½	6	9½	11½	15	19	22
Blue (M)	1¼	2½	4¼	6¼	9	12	15½	20	23
Yellow (F)	1½	2½	4	6½	9	11	13	17	20
White (F)	1¼	2	3	5	8	10	13	17	19½
Turquoise (F)	1	1	3	4	7	9	10½	14	18
Orange (M)	1¼	2½	4¼	6½	10	12½	17	21	24¼
Purple (M)	1½	2½	3	6¼	9	11	15	19	22

During the first weeks after delivery the bitch's temperature should be checked daily, and any dramatic elevation should be reported to the veterinarian. She will have a vaginal discharge for a few weeks and this should be checked to make sure that there is no evidence of infection. Her breasts must be palpated daily, to check for mastitis, an udder infection which is painful to the bitch and may poison the puppies. The bitch's breasts and vulva should be rinsed daily to keep them clean and to keep down the odor from the vaginal discharge. The whelping box should have clean padding for sanitation.

For weak or very small puppies, supplemental feeding is often recommended. One method is to use a standard baby bottle and preemie nipple; another is tube feeding with a catheter attached to a syringe. This latter method should be demonstrated by an experienced person. The commercially prepared puppy formulas are most convenient and are readily obtainable from a veterinarian or a pet supply store. At about three weeks of age supplemental feeding should be begun for all the puppies. The amount fed each day should be increased over a period of three weeks, until the puppies can be weaned completely. Start hand feeding each puppy individually. A recommended starter meal would be raw ground beef, about the size of a golf ball, with water added so that pups can suck it off your fingers. Gradually add puppy chow that has been soaked to a mush in hot water. Milk can be added as pups become competent eaters. Once they are able to eat without assistance, all the puppies can eat from a communal pan, but be sure that the small ones get their share. If they are pushed aside, feed them separately. Gradually increase the number of meals and cut back on the time the dam is allowed with her puppies. When the puppies are about six weeks old, they should be weaned completely. Four meals a day are sufficient from this time until the puppies are about ten weeks old, when they can be fed three meals a day. At six months feed twice a day. About the time the puppy reaches one year of age, feedings may be reduced to one each day plus a snack.

Puppies need to be moved to larger temporary quarters at around three weeks. Until they begin to eat solid food, the dam will eat their feces. Once on solid food, the whelping box quickly becomes fouled. At six weeks the pups can be moved to outdoor quarters with plenty of room to play and exercise. A dry, heated shelter is necessary in cold weather. Shelter from rain and sun is needed in warm weather. Needless to say, fencing is a must.

Once they are weaned, the puppies should be given parvovirus and temporary DHLP injections every two weeks until they are old enough for permanent inoculations. At three weeks, stool specimens should be checked for worms. Specimens should be checked again at five weeks, and as often thereafter as your veterinarian recommends.

Like humans, dogs may be born with heart defects. Newfoundlands are susceptible to congenital heart disease which may result in premature death as early as a few months of age. Puppies' hearts should be checked at the time of each vaccination by a veterinarian competent to diagnose cardiac disease. Puppies with suspicious murmurs should not be placed in new homes until, or unless, these murmurs "clear" at a later age.

Eight-week-old Pouch Cove puppies pay a call on a member of the younger generation, still in the whelping box.

This five-month-old puppy shows the "white undercoat" syndrome, the cause of which is unknown. The light color disappears when the adult coat is fully grown. Puppies should not be shown until the mixed coloring is gone.

Pedigree of Ch. Kilyka's Jupiter Rex, C.D., Ch. Kilyka's Black Bart, and American and Canadian Ch. Kilyka's Jessica of Pouch Cove, C.D.

Ch. Kilyka's Jupiter Rex, C.D. (pedigree at right).

Twelve-year-old American and Canadian Ch. Kilyka's Jessica of Pouch Cove, C.D. (pedigree at right), and Ch. Kilyka's Becky Jo of Pouch Cove.

Ch. Kilyka's Black Bart (pedigree at right).

				Ch. Dryad's Pilot
			Dryad's Anchorage of Waseeka	
				Waseeka's Harbor Light
		Dryad's Goliath of Gath		
				Topsails Leif Ericsson
			Dryad's Spinnaker	
				Oquaga's Sea Mist
	Ch. Dryad's Lord Nelson, U.D.T.			
				Oquaga's Sea Diver II
			Ch. Dryad's Sea Rover	
				Dryad's Sultana
		Dryad's Lake Rova		
				Dryad's Goliath of Gath
			Dryad's Helen of Troy, C.D.	
				Dryad's Miss Ebony

				Oquaga's Sea Diver II
			Ch. Dryad's Sea Rover	
				Dryad's Sultana
		Can. Ch. Dryad's Bounty		
				Ch. Perivale's Sea Ranger
			Dryad's Gumdrop	
				Dryad's Ocean Belle
	Ch. Shipshape's Sibyl, U.D.T.			
				Topsail's Captain Bob Bartlet
			Am. Can. & Ber. Ch. Newton	
				Merry of Sperry
		Ch. Dryad's Compass Rose		
				Ch. Dryad's Harborlight Lookout
			Dryad's Christmas Holly	
				Dryad's Bedelia

Bloodlines

As mentioned in an earlier chapter, much of the foundation for today's Newfoundlands originated with three Siki sons imported from England by Elizabeth Loring (Mrs. Davieson Power) of Waseeka Kennels. Waseeka Newfoundlands were prominent in pedigrees and in the show rings in the 1930s, '40s, and into the '50s. In the 1940s and '50s Dryad, Coastwise, and Little Bear Kennels became important forces in the breed, and much of their stock was based upon Waseeka bloodlines. Oquaga, Seaward, Irwindyl, and Moral View were also active during this period. Other United States kennel names found on older pedigrees include Carbonear, Harforidge, Harobed, Spinnaker, Temanend, and Top Gallant. Canadian kennel names from that era include Cedarbeck, Glenmire, Harbour Beem, Perivale, Shipmate, Westerland, and Top Sail.

In the mid-sixties, a "third generation" of breeders began. Kennels which rose to prominence in the late '60s, such as Edenglen, Shipshape, and Nashua-Auke were based largely on Dryad and/or Little Bear foundation stock. By 1970 the number of breeding kennels had increased greatly.

Two stud dogs figure prominently in the pedigrees of many top winning and top producing Newfoundlands since the late 1960s. They are Ch. Dryad's Sea Rover and Dryad's Goliath of Gath, both bred by Kitty and Maynard K. Drury. The pedigrees of these dogs include bloodlines from Dryad, Oquaga, Waseeka, Coastwise, and Top Sail Kennels. Of Newfoundlands taking the major wins at the Newfoundland Club of America National Specialty Show since 1967, most have one or both of these dogs listed in their pedigree. These dogs are found in the second and third generations of the earlier winners and are repeated frequently in the fourth to sixth generations of more recent winners.

Outstanding examples of such pedigrees are those of Ch. Kilyka's Jupiter Rex, C.D., owned by Fran and Bob Dibble; American and Canadian Ch. Kilyka's Jessica of Pouch Cove, C.D., owned by Peggy and David Helming; and Ch. Kilyka's Black Bart, owned by Betty McDonnell and Gerlinde Hockla. Sired by Ch. Dryad's Lord Nelson, U.D.T., ex Ch. Shipshape's Sibyl, U.D.T., these three dogs were bred by Betty McDonnell.

Jupiter was the 1971 National Specialty Best-of-Breed winner. At the same show, his younger brother Bart and sister Jessica won their respective Six-to-Nine Months Puppy Classes. At the 1976 National Specialty Jessica went Best of Opposite Sex, and Bart took Best of Breed at the 1979 National Specialty as a nine-year-old out of the Veterans Class. Bart is also an all breed Best-in-Show winner with many Group placements.

The pedigree of these dogs is on page 70. Note that Goliath of Gath is both grandsire and great-great-grandsire. Sea Rover is repeated as great-grandsire.

Ch. Seaward's Blackbeard, bred by Nancy McMahon and K. Lien, and owned by Elinor Ayers' Seaward Kennels, was the 1982 National Specialty Best-of-Breed winner. He has set a record for Newfoundland Best-in-Show (all breed) wins. Both Sea Rover and Goliath are in his pedigree as double great-great-grandsires.

American and Canadian Ch. Nor'west's Major Masquerador, bred and owned by Nancy Wheeler. Major has two all-breed Best-in-Show wins and multiple Group placements. He also is a Regional Specialty Best-of-Breed winner.

American and Canadian Ch. Little Bear's James Thurber, owned by Robert Dowling.

While neither Sea Rover nor Goliath was a top winner of his time, and Goliath indeed was never finished to a championship, both sired many outstanding champion get. Combined in pedigrees, they became a dominant force behind many of today's best Newfs.

In addition to the Nelson ex Sibyl breeding shown on page 70, there were other notable breedings combining Goliath and Rover. Ch. Dryad's Tambaram of Cayuga, a grandson of both dogs, was Best of Breed at the 1972 National Specialty, and his daughter, Ch. Niote of Newton-Ark, was Best of Opposite Sex in 1971. Tambaram was owned by Lynn and Edward Wilson. His brother, Ch. Dryad's George, owned by Elizabeth and William Stiles, produced 1970 National Specialty Best-of-Breed winner Ch. Edenglen's Falstaff, bred by Helena and Willie Linn and owned by Mr. and Mrs. J. B. Potts. Falstaff was out of Ch. Dryad's George ex Ch. Edenglen's Becky. In two litters, this combination produced eight champions from a total of eleven puppies. Falstaff and his brother Ch. Shalom Aleichem, owned by Nita and Don Jager, were among the top ten Newfoundlands for 1969.

Another well known litter, bred by Dorothy and James Bellows, combined Ch. Edenglen's Banner, 1968 and 1969 National Specialty Best-of-Breed winner, and a Rover son, with Ch. Dryad's Candy's Duchess, a Goliath daughter. This litter produced seven champions including Ch. Tranquilus Neptune, owned by Tranquilus Kennels and Penelope Buell. Neptune was one of the ten top winning Newfs during the years 1971 through 1974. Ch. Banner Dutch Baby from this litter produced multiple Best-in-Show winner Ch. Semy Egads Charlie, bred and owned by Luann Pingle. Semy Kennels' champion lines were based on Candy's Duchess stock.

An illustrious litter bred by Janet and Alan Levine and Ronnie Farkas combined Ch. Jack the Ripper, a Rover grandson, and Ch. Edenglen's Lady Rebecca, a Goliath granddaughter. This litter produced the following champions: Kuhaia's Rego, Pouch Cove Judd of Newton-Ark, The Sleeper of Newton-Ark, and Neshuma of Newton-Ark, as well as the unshown but popular stud dog, Loki's Drummer of Newton-Ark. Neshuma is the top winning Newfoundland bitch to date, with three Best-in-Show wins. Judd, Sleeper, and Rego have multiple Group wins and placements among them. These littermates have produced several National Specialty winners. The 1979 and 1983 Best-of-Opposite Sex winner, Ch. Ferryland's Abby of Newton-Ark, bred by Richard Swan and owned by the Levines, is out of Rego. Bred to The Sleeper, Abby produced Ch. Mogen of Newton-Ark, 1983 National Specialty Best-of-Breed winner. Ch. Pouch Cove Gref of Newton-Ark, bred by Peggy Helming and Janet Levine, and owned by Julie Heyward, was a Select winner sired by Rego. Mooncusser RSVP of Pouch Cove, another Select winner, bred by Suzanna Jones and D. Dodge and owned by the Helmings, was

Ch. Dryad's **Coastwise** Showboat, the first Newfoundland bitch to win an all-breed Best in Show (1949), was bred by Dryad Kennels and owned by Coastwise Kennels. Dryad and Coastwise Kennels perpetuated the excellent type of the Waseeka bloodlines.

American and Canadian Ch. Da Cody De Nashau-Auke, bred and owned by Jane and Ron Thibault. Cody is a multiple all-breed Best-in-Show winner, and Best-of-Breed winner of the 1977 NCA National Specialty.

Ch. Ferryland's Abby of Newton Ark, bred by Richard Swan and owned by Robin Seaman and Janet Levine. Abby was Best of Opposite Sex at the 1979 NCA National Specialty.

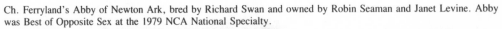

sired by Loki's Drummer. When their breeding records are completed, any or all of these Rip ex Rebecca sons should rank among the top producers of their time.

Betty McDonnell's Kilyka Kennels and the Helmings' Pouch Cove Kennels are based largely upon Goliath-Rover bloodlines. Both have Little Bear bloodlines scattered throughout their pedigrees, mainly through breedings to Nashua-Auke stock. Ch. Canicula Campio, bred and owned by Margaret and Vadim Chern, was a National Specialty Best-of-Breed winner in 1958 and 1961. His son, Ch. Little Bear's Dauntless, owned by Jane and Ron Thibault, was a foundation sire of their Nashua-Auke Kennels. He appears in the pedigrees of many well known Nashua-Auke champions and their champion progeny. The Thibaults very successfully combined the Little Bear and Dryad lines through Dauntless and Ch. Shipshape's Nana of Nashua-Auke.

An interesting pedigree is that of Motion Carried of Pouch Cove, bred and owned by the Helmings. At the 1982 National Specialty this bitch went Winners Bitch out of the Six-to-Nine Months Puppy Class. Her pedigree includes Rover and Goliath at least eleven times in the sixth and seventh generations. Canicula Campio also appears in her pedigree.

Canicula Campio is also behind other National Specialty winners. He was the sire of the 1964 winner, Ch. Little Bear's Thunder, U.D., bred by Little Bear Kennels and owned by Roger Richards. Ch. Black Molly of Warren, bred by A. and B. Restuccia and owned by Jean Goodrich, was Best of Opposite Sex in 1973. American and Canadian Ch. DaCody de Nashua-Auke, 1977 Best-of-Breed winnner, bred and owned by the Thibaults, and Ch. Hilvig's Corsage, 1968 Best-of-Opposite-Sex winner, bred and owned by Hilda Madsen, both have pedigrees combining Canicula Campio and Sea Rover.

Joan and Roger Foster's Halirock Kennels also combined Canicula Campio and Rover-Goliath. They began with foundation bitch Ch. Little Bear's Chulavista, a Canicula Campio granddaughter. Her second litter out of Ch. Edenglen's Beau Geste, a Sea Rover son, produced Ch. Halirock's Boulder, sire of several champions. The Fosters also acquired two Candy's Duchess daughters, Ch. Dryad's Anthony's Penelope and Ch. Franco Cassandra, who are also behind their many Halirock champions.

The list of the top twelve champion-producing Newfoundland sires from 1944 to 1975 includes Ch. Little Bear's Canicula Campio, Ch. Dryad's Sea Rover, and Dryad's Goliath of Gath. The top three on the list are Edenglen's Tucker, bred and owned by the Linns, Ch. Edenglen's Beau Geste, bred by the Linns and owned by the Dibbles, and Ch. Shipshape's Cutty Sark, bred and owned by Wilma and Bob Lister. These three dogs, plus four others on the list, were either direct descendants of, or were line bred on, Goliath and Rover.

American, Canadian, and Bermudian Ch. Newton, bred in Newfoundland at the Westerland Kennels of the Hon.

American and Canadian Ch. Seamount Compass North, bred and owned by Jo Ann and Alan Riley.

Three proud owners pose with their new puppy just before taking it home.

Ch. Shipshape's Sibyl, U.D.T., bred by Christine Lister and owned by Betty McDonnell, is the top producing bitch in Newfoundland History, with fourteen champion get, including two National Specialty Best-of-Breed winners.

Ch. Dryad's Lord Nelson, U.D.T., bred by Lily Fulton and owned by Betty McDonnell. Nelson was the first U.D.T.-titled Newf. He sired two National Specialty Best-of-Breed winners as well as numerous champions and obedience titled Newfs.

Ch. Edenglen's Oscar, bred by Edenglen Kennels and owned by Fran and Bob Dibble. Oscar was the sire of some thirty champions, and was a Regional Specialty Best-of-Breed winner, and an all-breed-show Group winner.

American and Canadian Ch. Neshuma of Newton Ark, bred by Janet Levine and Ronnie Farkas and owned by Kathi and Curt Sahner. Neshuma was Best of Winners at the 1974 NCA National Specialty and is the only Newf bitch to win three all breed Best-in-Show awards.

Fencing and space for exercise are important for the safety and health of house pets.

Harold McPherson, while not on the list of top producers, appears on many of the fine pedigrees which trace back to the mid-sixties.

Other outstanding sires whose breeding records were not completed at the time the 1975 list of top producers was compiled are Ch. Edenglen's Oscar, bred by the Linns and owned by the Dibbles, and Ch. Edenglen's Sovereign of the Sea, bred by the Linns and owned by Isabelle and William Kurth. This dog out of Sea Rover had produced several champion get as of 1976, including Ch. Indigo's Fritzacker, bred and owned by Pauline and Myron O'Neill. Fritz was the 1973 National Specialty Best-of-Breed winner and was the sire of multiple Best in Show winner Ch. Canooche de Nashua-Auke, who was bred and owned by the Thibaults.

Top producing dams of the 1944–1975 era included Ch. Shipshape's Sibyl, Ch. Edenglen's Becky, Ch. Edenglen's Lady Rebecca, and Ch. Dryad's Candy's Duchess. Among the eleven champion progeny of Candy's Duchess was the 1969 National Specialty Best-of-Breed winner, Ch. Tranquilus Betty of Subira, owned by Penelope Stucky (formerly Penelope Buell) of Peppertree Kennels.

Ch. Dryad's Nancy of Glenora, bred by the Drurys and owned by the Linns, produced among her ten champion get the outstanding sires Ch. Edenglen's Beau Geste and Ch. Edenglen's Sovereign of the Sea.

There are many Newfoundland breeders who have contributed to the breed through their Newfoundlands that have won titles in the conformation ring, and in obedience and Water Test competition. Although championship titles are only one measure of a breed's greatness, we have dwelt here on well known champions and their progeny because these dogs have had the most profound influence on the breed through wide dissemination of their genes.

Four-generation pedigrees of the future will no longer show the important bloodlines and outstanding sires and dams of the earlier and more recent past. Certain contemporary sires and dams will begin to double up in the fourth, fifth, and sixth generation spaces, indicating their strong influences on the Newfoundland breed. But the past is also the future for all living things, and the heritage from the earlier breeders and their stock will always be a part of living Newfoundlands.

The 1985 National Specialty Best-of-Breed winner, Ch. Tuckamore's Julie, bred and owned by Barbara Finch. Left to right are: John White, Show Co-chairman; Betty McDonnell, NCA President; Jo Ann Riley, BOB judge; and Louis Grello, handling Ch. Tuckamore's Julie.

These Denlinger books available in local stores, or write the publisher.

YOUR DOG BOOK SERIES

Illustrated with photographs and line drawings, including chapters on selecting a puppy, famous kennels and dogs, breed history and development, personality and character, training, feeding, grooming, kenneling, breeding, whelping, etc. 5½ x 8½.

YOUR AFGHAN HOUND
YOUR AIREDALE TERRIER
YOUR ALASKAN MALAMUTE
YOUR BASENJI
YOUR BEAGLE
YOUR BORZOI
YOUR BOXER
YOUR BULLDOG
YOUR BULL TERRIER
YOUR CAIRN TERRIER
YOUR CHIHUAHUA
YOUR DACHSHUND
YOUR ENGLISH SPRINGER SPANIEL
YOUR GERMAN SHEPHERD
YOUR GERMAN SHORTHAIRED POINTER
YOUR GREAT DANE

YOUR LHASA APSO
YOUR MALTESE
YOUR MINIATURE PINSCHER
YOUR NORWEGIAN ELKHOUND
YOUR OLD ENGLISH SHEEPDOG
YOUR PEKINGESE
YOUR POMERANIAN
YOUR POODLE
YOUR PUG
YOUR SAMOYED
YOUR SHIH TZU
YOUR SILKY TERRIER
YOUR ST. BERNARD
YOUR VIZSLA
YOUR WELSH CORGI
YOUR YORKSHIRE TERRIER

OTHER DOG BOOKS

THE BEARDED COLLIE
THE BELGIAN SHEEPDOG
BIRD DOGS AND UPLAND GAME BIRDS
THE BOOK OF DOG GENETICS
THE BOSTON TERRIER
THE BOUVIER DES FLANDRES
BREEDING BETTER COCKER SPANIELS
THE BRITTANY
THE BULLMASTIFF
THE CARDIGAN HANDBOOK
THE CHESAPEAKE BAY RETRIEVER
CHINESE NAMES FOR ORIENTAL DOGS
THE CHINESE SHAR-PEI
THE COMPLETE GERMAN SHORTHAIRED POINTER
DOG OBEDIENCE TRAINING MANUAL, VOL. 1
DOG OBEDIENCE TRAINING MANUAL, VOL. 2
DOG OBEDIENCE TRAINING MANUAL, VOL. 3
DOGS IN SHAKESPEARE
DOGS ON THE FRONTIER
DOG TRAINING IS KID STUFF
DOG TRAINING IS KID STUFF COLORING BOOK
THE DYNAMICS OF CANINE GAIT
GAELIC NAMES FOR CELTIC DOGS
GERMAN NAMES FOR GERMAN DOGS
THE GOLDEN RETRIEVER
THE GREAT AMERICAN DOG SHOW GAME

GREAT DANES IN CANADA
GROOMING AND SHOWING TOY DOGS
GUIDE TO JUNIOR SHOWMANSHIP
HOW TO SPEAK DOG
HOW TO TRAIN DOGS FOR POLICE WORK
THE IRISH TERRIER
THE KERRY BLUE TERRIER
THE LABRADOR RETRIEVER
LEADER DOGS FOR THE BLIND
THE MASTIFF
MEISEN BREEDING MANUAL
MEISEN POODLE MANUAL
MR. LUCKY'S TRICK DOG TRAINING
THE NEWFOUNDLAND
THE PHARAOH HOUND
THE PORTABLE PET
RAPPID OBEDIENCE & WATCHDOG TRAINING
RUSSIAN NAMES FOR RUSSIAN DOGS
SHOW DOGS—PREPARATION AND PRESENTATION OF
SKITCH (The Message of the Roses)
THE STANDARD BOOK OF DOG BREEDING
THE STANDARD BOOK OF DOG GROOMING
THE STANDARD BOOK OF KENNEL MANAGEMENT
TOP PRODUCERS—SIBERIAN HUSKYS
THE UNCOMMON DOG BREEDS
YOU AND YOUR IRISH WOLFHOUND

To order any of these books, write to Denlinger's Publishers, P.O. Box 76, Fairfax, VA 22030

For information call (703) 631-1500

VISA and Master Charge orders accepted.

New titles are constantly in production, so please call us to inquire about breed books not listed here.